a

Song

in my heart

By R. Douglas Veer and Kathy Veer

Changed Lives Publishing, LLC

2023

First Printing: 2023
ISBN-13: 978-1-7323243-6-7
Library of Congress Control Number: 2023900458

Cover Design: K. Veer
Photo Credits
Music Sheet Notes: https://pixabay.com/photos/music-sheet-notes-melody-pattern-6293305/
Photo of Kathy Veer:
Courtesy 2nd Baptist Church; Thomson, GA 30824

Scripture Versions are abbreviated;
i.e. King James noted as KJV.

* * * * * * *

Book Ordering: Amazon.com
Booking Information, please visit
www.KathyVeer.com or www.DougVeer.com

Changed Lives Publishing, LLC
Region of Augusta, Georgia

YOUR OPINION COUNTS!

If you have enjoyed
this book,
please consider
**writing a short
book review
at Amazon.com**

Help us spread the word,
and share Jesus

INTRODUCTION

MY STORY BEGINS . . .

The freezing temperatures and the slashing winds bit hard at Mom and Dad as they hurried through the bitter Canadian weather, fearing for the life of their two-year-old daughter. She needed serious medical attention and they were rushing her to the hospital with her 104-degree fever. They wondered if their little one would survive or if they'd lose her along the way.

Panic and fear gripped them as they zig-zagged through busy Montreal traffic. Would they make it? Would the doctors know what to do? Could they finally break her burning fever?

Heavy wind-driven snow was piling up in the streets making driving a slippery task but time was of the essence. No matter *what,* they *had* to get through. Their little girl's life was at stake.

Her parents' hearts were thundering like wayward drums, beating with love for their child as they cried out for help. Were they doing everything they could? Would Old Father Time take her away from them? These were the questions they wrestled with while hoping for a miracle. Where was their guardian angel?

The angels must have been helping because they did arrive in time for all the poison to be pulled out of her tiny, two-year-old body. She hovered on the brink of death as the doctors discovered her tonsils had burst. Their diagnosis was correct. They managed the case well and they took good care of her.

But would this be her last life-threatening scare? Would this be her last anxious brush with death? No. The years ahead would be one continual battle after another before she would find her purpose and true place in life; a time when she'd be able to say, "I have a song in my heart."

CHAPTER ONE

DO THINGS EVER CHANGE

I was born during the August heat in the city of Montreal, Quebec, in eastern Canada. It's a time that brings on sweltering temperatures. But to be quite honest, it's a welcome time of year compared to the frigid cold that grips the city during the winter months.

While summers were pleasant, those cold clouds of despair would soon be coming to hang over me like an ever-present cloak, constantly driving me to search for warmth and protection wherever I could.

Would things ever change? I hoped so. I hoped I could change my destiny as easily as I had changed my name from Kathleen to Kathy. Well, I didn't actually change it; I thought Kathleen was rather old-fashioned and I preferred the shorter, more comfortable version. It helped me better fit in with the crowd.

What's Montreal like? Besides being downright cold with many chilly periods for six or seven months, there are plenty of damp, wet days, too. Mmm. Was this a foretelling of my future?

Since my young life was just beginning, could these miserable conditions be an introduction to the rest of my existence? Would my life always be a bitter fight? Time, in its often unkind way, would have to pass before such answers would be revealed.

FROM HUNGARY WITH LOVE

During the 1950s, Canada was a melting pot of a myriad of nationalities coming to the region, mirroring what it was like in the U.S. during the early 1900s.

Jozsef Debreceni was one of those who came to Montreal from Hungary to escape communist rule, also known as the Hungarian Revolution. That was in 1956, a few years before I was born.

Back in Budapest, my yet unmarried father, Joe, had been an exceptionally skilled tool and die maker. He had a very good trade to rely on for his livelihood. So, he abandoned the uprising and came to Canada with just a file and a micrometer, and about ten dollars in his pocket. There, he walked the busy streets of Montreal, looking for work.

With the kind of determination and work ethic he brought with him from the "old country," he and his good friend, Leslie (who had traveled over later) were determined to make good in this land of promise.

After working a few years for others and applying his talents for financial benefit, Joe took the gamble and started his own manufacturing business in the plastics/injection mold trade. With little money backing him, his skills and hard work made up for what he lacked financially, and his reputation grew.

Soon, this man who once desperately looked for work himself now began looking for other skilled people, offering them opportunities to work for him.

In the midst of all that, Joe met a young woman, Rosetta Rule, who everyone called "Rosie." They fell in love, and in 1958, became husband and wife. Rosie dreamed of having a little girl and a year or so later God answered her prayers. On the day of August 20, 1959, Kathleen, the daughter of Joe and Rosetta, was born. That was me.

WHITE PEPPERMINTS

My dad's parents and my mother's parents were an interesting lot. My dad never knew his real father. He left when my dad was born, so my dad was raised by a stepfather.

When my dad was still a young boy, his stepfather passed away so his mother continued to raise him on her own. She was a very smart and talented lady. I'll introduce her to you in the next chapter.

My mother's parents, George and Rosetta Rule, came to Montreal from England on their honeymoon. They loved Canada so much that they never went back to their homeland. They settled in Montreal where my mother and her two brothers were born. For me that was great. I had a wonderful set of grandparents close by and a few cousins, too.

When I was a child we used to visit my mother's parents fairly often. I have some happy memories of those times. I especially loved being with my grandad. I loved when he played the piano; it fascinated me.

Besides that, he always had a pocket full of little white peppermints which he would share. (I thought he kept them handy just for me.)

We use to play ring-around-the-Rosie; then we'd "all fall down" and laugh and giggle. Then he'd slip me a couple of peppermints. Today, that memory is still crystal clear.

BLOOMFIELD STREET

Bloomfield Street in Montreal was the first place I remember living. I was very young but I have pictures in my mind of our living room and the street outside. That was a hard time in my life because I almost died when my tonsils burst; I was just a baby.

Mom and Dad rushed me to the hospital with a 104-degree fever and made it there just in time. They cleared all the poison out of my system and kept me for a few days for observation.

I didn't like being in the hospital at all and I let them know it. (They don't call it the "terrible two's" for nothing.) They said that one evening I threw my

3

supper at the nurse. It included a bowl of cooked, green peas. You know, I sort of remember that . . .

I built many memories through the years, even from an early age. They fit together like an intricate stone wall, one piece at a time. I guess we all have memories we can look back on; some good, some bad, and some just plain unusual. But these were my building blocks and they've never left me. Now that I'm an adult I'm very grateful for them.

THE NOT-SO-GOOD MEMORIES

To me, my dad was always bigger than life. I somehow glorified him. But I also learned very early on that I could easily displease and upset him. His words could be harsh and sometimes came with physical discipline.

He would always explain the principles behind his reprimands because he wanted me to pay attention, to learn, to succeed, and to overcome weaknesses. Once in a while, however, he would misunderstand my words or actions. I wasn't able to explain myself and the consequences were severe.

I remember when I was between the ages of two and three, we went to a country place on a weekend outing. My dad went fishing and came back hours later with several fish hooked to a line he was carrying.

I looked up at him, smiling, and said, "Black bass." But my dad thought I said a bad word. He went into a rage and screamed at me. He said, "Don't you *ever* call me that, not *ever!*" (He thought I called him a b*st*rd.) And then he spanked me, hard.

That weekend I became very ill with an upper respiratory infection. There weren't any doctors or

4

medicines available so they applied hot mustard cloths to my chest and hoped I would get better. I did recover after a good couple of weeks.

WHAT IF?

On a lighter note, I was three years old when we moved into a second-floor apartment on Carlton Street. I enjoyed living there and it was there that I began my crazy "what if" adventures; they *were* quite unusual.

What do I mean by, "what if?" Anytime I had a thought about something, I would try it. They were crazy things like, "What if I stuck my finger in here?" or "What if I packed all of this stuff in my mouth at once?"

My crazy "what ifs" went on and on for years, generally ending in one disaster after another. Like when I was riding my bike one day, I wondered what would happen if I turned the wheel sideways while rolling downhill. Duh . . . Lying in a heap over that same wheel is how I found out what would happen. To this day, I still have a scar on my knee from that little lesson.

The entrance door to our Carlton Street apartment building was at the end of a short walkway. Once past the outer door, there was a hallway to the left that went to the main-floor apartment. Then to the right was a stairway to the upstairs where we lived. There was also a back entrance that had a long two-story set of steps.

I remember wondering what would happen if I tried pulling my little doll carriage up those back steps. Well, that "what if" got the best of me. While pulling the carriage upwards, the weight pulled me back down. The carriage and I tumbled head over heels all the way to the bottom. Or should I say, "head over wheels?"

Thankfully, on the way up, I had only reached the seventh or eighth step but I still got pretty banged up from the fall. The bruises left me after a few weeks but the memory never will.

Many years later I took my husband, Doug, on a tour of my childhood neighborhoods in Montreal. Those steps were one of the places we visited so I told him the story.

There were other "what if" occasions but I never learned; I never stopped trying. I've been plagued with this silliness all my life and each new adventure has added more building blocks to my wall of memories.

THE OLD MAN WITH THE WOOLY BEARD

My mother would tell me about God sometimes. She did not have a personal relationship with Him but she believed there was a God up in heaven somewhere, looking down upon the whole world.

My dad believed there was a God, too, but he made no mention of Him in any sort of serious way. Suffice it to say, my dad was not an atheist.

I had a little plastic wading pool that my mom would put out on the back landing, just outside our kitchen door. In the summertime, she would fill it up with water for me to splash around in.

I would sit in it for hours in the hot sun watching the clouds drift by, wondering if God was hiding behind them. I thought He must be quite old and most likely had a big wooly beard that looked just like the clouds.

I hoped that God liked little children. I often felt nobody liked me and viewed me as ugly. Yes, people made me feel that way. I knew my mom loved me and my dad probably did too, even though he was mad at me a lot.

I was a daydreamer and didn't pay attention well. Dad had stern words about that. He didn't like the way I colored pictures, either. He said I was always going outside the lines.

He was very precise in his line of work. I guess he wanted me to grow up with the same kind of attention to detail. He only wanted the best for me. I just wished it didn't have to hurt so much.

CHAPTER TWO

MY STEREO

Aside from sad thoughts, I have some pleasant memories, too, like the stereo console we had in the living room. It had a nice cabinet that housed a radio and a record player.

I was already becoming a loner and instead of going outside to play with other kids, I chose to lay on the sofa for hours listening to stacks of records in our collection. I spent days cuddled up to that speaker, listening to tunes.

It was the mid-1960s and the music was great back then. I loved all the popular songs; some of my favorite styles were jazz and blues sung by the old black female singers. There was something magical about their singing that crawled up and nestled into my soul.

But I listened to everything from pop to big bands, to country and western. As long as it was good music, I could get lost in it for hours. That was unusual for a three or four-year-old.

Of course, being an only child didn't help my social skills but my love for music only added to my desire to be alone.

The yelling and laughter of the other kids running and playing outside my window never drew me in as music did. It was like a magnet. I couldn't get enough of it.

My secret wish was to make my own music one day. It cried out for release from deep within but I never told anyone about it because I didn't understand what it was.

AN ENCOURAGING GIFT

Then, as if by the hand of some great power far above, bigger than anything I could imagine, my mom bought me a miniature, white, upright piano. It had authentic keys and it played like the real thing. Wow!

I wanted to make music on it; not make-believe music like other kids, but real music with melody and feeling that made sense . . . like on the radio. I wanted to live the dreams that had captivated me.

I hoped to have lessons so I could learn how to play, but for some reason that never happened. Maybe it cost too much money? I was disappointed, for sure, but I had to let it go and wait until *time* would bring other opportunities.

Just having that piano, though, made me feel special. It fueled more daydreams of my being a musician one day. Those imaginary chains would be unlocked and I'd be released to make sounds, bringing unspeakable joy to my heart. I imagined musical notes dancing in the air, touching others as well as myself.

Time held the key to all of that. And somehow, some way, I'd manage to find the patience to wait . . . which was the hardest thing of all.

NAGYMAMA

At about that time, my grandmother, (my father's mother), came from Hungary to live with us. The word for Grandmother in Hungarian is "Nagymama" which is pronounced, "nyud-ma-ma."

My grandmother spoke hardly any English so she taught me to speak Hungarian. She would walk around the house pointing to objects and would give me the Hungarian word for each item. Through our made-up sign language and a few grunts here and there, I learned to communicate with her in about three months' time.

As I got older I became very fluent; it was like a second native language. I could translate for some of our Hungarian friends who needed someone to bridge the English gap. And my dad said I learned the language so well, I could even understand the jokes.

My grandmother could be very serious and firm but she was not without a sense of humor. One day while she was mixing some batter, the bowl broke and its contents ran down the side of the cupboard. She thought it was hilarious. We both hit the floor and laughed until we cried.

Nagymama was a good cook and was also very skilled at sewing and crocheting. She sometimes made clothes for my Barbie doll and even created some outfits for our poodle.

My mother used to tell the story about how one day, she had taken the dog for a walk. The little thing was all dressed up in Grandmother's overcoat, hat, tiny red socks, and boots. At one point, a certain truck driver passed by. But when he saw the dog, he had to pull over because he was laughing so hard.

Yes, Nagymama was a good woman and very talented. Sadly, I never did learn much from her in the way of household skills like most girls do. I guess music had absorbed me, filling my mind and it left no room for those other kinds of things.

THERE'S A STRING ATTACHED

That same year at Christmas time my dad gave me the most precious gift. It was a "Bozo the Clown." He was all dressed up in his colorful, blue, polka-dot outfit contrasted by his bright orange hair that fluffed out around the crown of his head leaving a bald spot.

Dad held the string behind Bozo's back so I couldn't see it, and to my delight, the amazing clown talked! Then Dad showed me how it worked and told me to take care of it and that I should never pull the string too hard. And I didn't.

Sometimes when company came and their kids came with them, I always asked my mother to hide my clown on the top shelf of the closet so they couldn't touch it. I was afraid they might break it.

I did just as my daddy said. I looked after my Bozo like a treasure. Now, here I am six decades later and I still have my Bozo. It sits on the top of my bedroom dresser where no harm can befall him. And yes, he can still talk.

THE CHOCOLATE MONSTER

I was only four years old when I bought my first candy bar. I walked to the store at the end of my street by myself and there, spent my own allowance money. I remember that it only cost three cents. It was called a "Nutmilk" bar, and it was really big. That day, I fell in love with chocolate.

For Easter that year I received a chocolate bunny as tall as me and I ate the whole thing. No, don't get excited. It didn't weigh ten or twenty pounds. It was hollow. But there were consequences to be paid and that price was a terrible one.

By the end of the year, I had so many cavities that I was taken to the hospital for an outpatient procedure. They put me to sleep and filled several of my teeth all at one time. It took them three hours to do the repairs. I guess the chocolate monster got the best of me.

THE COUNTRY PLACE

My dad went fishing every chance he could, and each summer we would spend our weekends at a cottage by a lake just west of Montreal in a place called Rigaud, (pronounced "Ree-go").

There weren't usually any children around so I would hang out with the guys, mostly, while they sat around playing cards and drinking "Fritch," (wine and soda water).

When I grew tired of watching them I would grab a broom and sweep the cabin, putting things in order. That compulsion has affected me throughout my life. I'm an extremely well-organized person; I love cleaning.

When I got tired of that I would go down to the lake and splash around in the shallow parts near the shore. I enjoyed the water and the sunshine.

My dad was a "super-achiever" and he wanted to raise me to be one, too. One day, after he'd played several card games, he decided to walk down to the peer to see what the women were doing.

When he saw me splashing around in ankle-deep water, he grabbed me up in his arms, walked down to the end of the boat dock, and threw me in.

All the while he was muttering, "You're going to "blankety-blank" learn how to swim if it kills me!" Then he walked away and left me in the water which was over my head.

Some people would think that was funny. What's the big deal, right? Lots of kids learn how to swim that way. My mother didn't think it was too cute. She started hollering at him while motioning for someone to get me out of there; (she couldn't swim either).

I don't remember who went in after me and I'm sure I had a few gulps of lake water before it was all over but I was okay. I didn't drown or anything although I was quite shaken. I wasn't too confident around water after that. (By the way, I would *never* suggest anyone do this to a child.)

I still went fishing with my dad after that but I was always leery of being in the boat, even with a life jacket on.

Once, when we were out in our little boat, we ventured toward the dam. A storm came up and suddenly we were caught in the middle of it.

I remember how scary that was because we had to maneuver around the whirlpools while fighting the high winds. My dad managed to get us back to shore safely but I viewed it as a close call.

In later years when I would visit, my dad would invite me to go fishing. I would go to please him but it *irked* him when I caught more fish than he did. One time, I even caught more fish than his professional fishing guide. They couldn't figure out how I did it. Neither could I but we laughed about it many times.

I have several more memories of when I was four; all of those experiences went into shaping who I would become. At this time, all I could think of was my next undertaking: starting public school.

CHAPTER THREE

THAT AWFUL FIRST DAY

Our neighbors--a nice Jewish family--had a daughter who was much older than me but we got along very well. Once in a while, I'd go to her house to visit and they would tell me about their special Jewish feasts like Hanukkah, for example, also known as the "Festival of Lights." They used a special candle holder they had called a "Menorah," and they served special foods. Even at that age, I found it very interesting.

When I turned five it was time to start kindergarten, so the daughter would walk me to school to make sure I arrived there safely. (I think she was going into grade six at the time.)

I'll never forget my first school day. I remember that Mom bought me a pretty pink, leather school bag to carry, so off I went into the big wide world like some executive.

My class lasted only a couple of hours, from nine until noon, but wouldn't you know it, around eleven o'clock, I had to go to the bathroom. Unfortunately, the girl's bathroom was out of order, so they told me to go into the boy's bathroom.

I did *not* want to do that. (I have always been "funny" about bathrooms . . . ask my husband), so I went in there but I didn't "go" because that bathroom was for boys.

I went back to my chair and about twenty minutes later there were giggles all around me. The other kids were laughing at me because there was a big puddle under my chair. Yes, you guessed it: I wet my pants. Oh what an awful first day that was.

LUNCH WAS ON ME

A year of school passed. The girl that walked me to school could no longer do it because she'd be attending a different school for grade seven. My mother wanted me to be independent anyway, so she walked me to school one Saturday to teach me how to cross the street by myself.

It was a big, busy intersection but being so young I didn't understand enough to be concerned about traffic.

When we got to the curb I immediately stepped right off the sidewalk into the street and my mother had to jerk me back. Oh yeah, I was quite properly scolded and I got a major lecture about paying attention and about being careful. Mom made it as clear as she could that this was no time for daydreaming, (my favorite past-time).

After I had learned to navigate the street alone, Mom released me to go off by myself when Monday rolled around. All was fine in the days and weeks to follow.

After a month or so, I started noticing the lunch counter inside a drugstore I passed, near the school. So, when lunchtime came, I fought my way across the traffic to get back over there.

I looked around inside the store and decided I might like to have lunch there instead of brown-bagging it. So, my mother opened an expense account for me and every Friday she would come in to pay the bill.

It was a great plan and it worked well for a while but in time, the bill got to be as high as twenty dollars which was a lot of money back then. After all, how much could a six-year-old eat?

Well, the truth was, I would order great big club sandwiches with fries and not even eat half of it. And

15

then I started inviting a friend or two to come with me and I'd treat them.

My mother was amazed when she found out what was going on. She had to get hold of my senses. Even so, she let me carry on a while longer and then finally cut me off. I guess it was good while it lasted.

During that tour of my old stomping grounds, this drugstore was another stop along the way I showed my husband. I told him about the big bills Mom had to pay and how Mom and I laughed about it in later years. What a silly young girl I was.

I also took Doug across the street to my old schoolyard. Just standing there reminded me of how I used to run and play. I especially liked chasing after a boy named Kevin. He had blonde hair and blue eyes and he was just dreamy.

My husband laughed when I told him the story. He said, "It's a good thing I have blonde hair and blue eyes." Yes, God knew my heart when he brought my husband into my life.

DRIVING MISS ROSIE

Aside from having to pay my *out-of-control* lunch expenses, Mom thought it was time for her to get a job and stretch her wings a bit. She wanted to earn a little spending money and get out of the house for a while so, she applied for a job at the Jewish General Hospital in Montreal. They hired her and she worked there for about three years.

During that time Mom bought a car and took driving lessons. It was a sweet, red, Chevrolet, Corvair convertible with a white leather interior. She loved that little car and enjoyed taking me for rides on the weekends.

There was only one teeny problem. She got lost everywhere she went. So inevitably, at the end of our excursions, she would always have to call my dad to come and find us and escort us home.

MOVING ON UP

In the spring of 1966, my father decided it was time to buy a house. By now his business was doing quite well. He owned a factory and had several employees and a few major contracts with companies like Electro-Lux, for example. He manufactured all the plastic parts for their vacuum cleaners. The business generated good money so, we definitely could afford to move out of our apartment on Carlton Street.

The three of us drove out to the suburb of Ville Brossard one weekend. The area was just beginning to develop and we viewed many show homes there. I remember how we walked up and down several blocks of that street to look at all the available houses. Finally, my parents picked one and bought it. It was a nice house; my father stayed there for the rest of his life.

GREEN, GREEN GRASS OF HOME

That summer, Mom and Dad and I moved into our new house along with my father's mother. Nagymama had her own room and so did I. My parents took the bedroom in the basement. That may not sound like much but it was a very nice room with a bathroom and other conveniences that gave them a private place to be.

We also had a nice living room upstairs with French Provincial-styled furniture. And just off of the dining room, we had a back porch with steps going down to a large grass-covered yard for me to run around in.

We had a big single-car garage that you could access from the basement and it became my place of play. I would set up my little portable record player there and play 78s, 45s, and 33 RPM records for hours at a time, listening to everything from Dean Martin to Sarah Vaughn, Hank Williams, and the Platters. I even listened to the Chipmunks and the funny songs they sang. They were all so wonderful.

We had two dogs that shared our house: a toy poodle and a red, Irish Setter. We didn't keep the Setter because he would chew holes in the walls and that didn't go over well. We kept the poodle though, whom we called "Chee Chee." He was the love of our lives.

From Spring through to the Fall our weekends continued to be filled with trips to the country house. Sometimes we'd go visit the cabin manager there. He always had a warm fire going in that pot-bellied stove of his. It was so cozy when the evening air got chilly.

Dad had other hunting and fishing buddies he used to go see. A lot of times it was just me and him that went visiting. I always enjoyed tagging along.

FAMILY

On special occasions, we would go visit my Aunt Norma and Uncle George. They had three children: a son, Doug, and two daughters, Pam and Linda.

Pam and Linda were about 13 years older than me. But Doug was closer to my age. When I was six years old, he was nine.

We enjoyed playing together. He had a neat room. He liked to build model airplanes and had a lot of them hanging from his ceiling. I always thought he was so clever.

I also remember us playing outside when it was hot. The house he lived in was part of a new development, so there was a lot of vacant land across the street. For a time, there was a giant slide there; it seemed like it was two stories high. We would climb up and slide down spending big chunks of time in our little park until the mosquitoes came out. Then we'd head inside for some lemonade.

I don't mean to be prejudiced, but Doug was always my favorite cousin . . . and we still keep in touch.

His mom passed away a couple of years ago; I tried sharing Jesus with her several times but she never seemed interested.

During her final hours in the hospital, Doug asked her if she was ready to accept Jesus Christ as her Lord and Savior. She said, "Yes." I'm so glad because she is safe and well and one day, we will all be together again!

NANA

After some time, my mother's mother, Nana, came to live with us. She was becoming rather senile and was almost bedridden so Nagymama had to take care of her. She was a real handful and quite a concern.

Caring for Nana was hard work; Nana needed a lot of attention. But Nagymama made it all happen. Of course, to a young girl like me, it was easy because it was someone else doing the work.

As a family, we were thriving. Dad's business continued to grow and I was also growing and becoming a gangly young girl with long skinny legs, and arms that flew this way and that. Years ago, Daddy nicknamed me "Szúnyog" which in his native language means, "mosquito."

I, Szúnyog, grew bigger and taller, but sadly, the bonds of marriage between my mother and father grew shorter as they grew farther apart.

Our household was a troubled place and as a seven-year-old, I was very upset about it. The arguing and the yelling escalated and it made me want to run away. So I did . . . well, sort of.

I found a big stick outside and tied a big kerchief to it as I had seen them do in the cartoons. I wasn't sure what I should put in it but I figured I needed food so I packed some sandwiches and cookies for later and then I headed down the street.

I wanted to cross the Champlain Bridge which was a couple of miles from my house. Oh, but how frail are the plans of mice and men. I didn't get far; just a few blocks. Then I turned around and came home.

The situation continued at my house and when my parents couldn't be committed to each other anymore, the marriage ended. My mother took me and we moved out of our family home. The life we were accustomed to was now going to change.

CHAPTER FOUR

MOVING OUT

Yes, my mother was devastated but what about me? I had no more Daddy, and no more home to feel secure in. I was lost in a world of adults whom I loved. Their mistreatment of each other was something I couldn't understand. All the while I kept wishing it was a dream.

My mother started drinking which was so out of character for her. Normally she had a sweet, pleasant personality but booze made her nasty-mouthed and the grief made her eyelids sag from all the crying.

Since she worked at the hospital, she sought a good plastic surgeon who fixed her eyes and put her lids back where they were supposed to be.

Months passed and my mother continued to work at the Jewish General Hospital. Our first apartment together was a one-room suite on Barclay Street, not far from Carlton where we used to live. We were there for six months or less.

Then, she found a bigger apartment across from the hospital on Cote Des Neige. An extra benefit was that she could walk to work and I could walk to school from there. It was a good distance but there were a couple of great candy stores along the way where I'd stop in after classes. Oh boy, more chocolate.

I don't remember having friends to play with, but we had a storage locker in the underground parkade. I used to play there on the concrete floor in the dust. I would take my radio down there and listen to it.

There were so many hits in those days: songs like, *Love is Blue, Dock of the Bay, Sunshine of Your Love, This Guy's in love With You, Mrs. Robinson, Harper Valley PTA, Hey Jude,* and many more. I loved them all.

ALEX

I didn't mind being alone, but it was worrisome knowing that my mom was having a hard time working, keeping house, and taking care of me, too. It was physically and emotionally difficult for her but she hung in there for my sake.

To make things worse, I started stealing. First, I took stuff from the drugstore. Then I started going to Woolworth's across from my school. I liked "View Master" discs. You could get different themes like nature, comic characters like *The Flintstones*, or old-fashioned stories like *Snow White and the Seven Dwarfs*. For a while, I got away with snatching them.

In the meantime, my mother befriended a man she had met a couple of years earlier at the hospital. He was some kind of supervisor and he admired her from a distance until one day he finally let her know he liked her.

She explained that she was married so that was the end of that until he caught wind of the news that she was getting a divorce. When he heard that, he started asking her to go out with him.

When Alex and my mother went out on dates they always took me. The three of us would ride in his fancy car with the electric windows.

Sometimes we'd go out to eat, sometimes we went to the movies, and sometimes he would come over to visit us and we'd have nice evenings together. He was a lot of fun and I was very fond of him, especially when he gave me piggyback rides.

For Christmas that year I knitted him a scarf, using the skills taught to me by my mother. But it was full of holes because I had dropped several stitches.

Also, it had a button for fastening it against his neck but using it almost choked him because the scarf was too short. Well, it was the best I could do. Even so, he kept that scarf for years and years. It was special to him.

Life was changing, but unfortunately, I was still stealing. Mom and Alex somehow figured it out and they kindly confronted me. So I came clean and admitted my crimes.

They gave me a serious talking to and as for my punishment, they made me go to Woolworths with them and confess my sins to the manager. Then my mother paid the man for the merchandise and deducted it from my allowance . . . well, for a while, until they finally let me off the hook.

TIME TO MOVE

My mother started feeling like she wanted to get away from Montreal. She talked to Alex about it and even though he had a good job, he was willing to give it up to please her. To my surprise, they decided to move to Toronto.

The two cities are about 300 miles apart. We didn't know anyone there except for a couple my mom kept in touch with. Even so, we packed up our belongings and moved six hours away, ending up in a rooming house on North Dufferin Street. That was the beginning of many places we would live.

Alex didn't stay in the hospital business. He did odd jobs for a while and then he and mom started managing apartment buildings. It was a brand new kind of life and quite stressful because we moved over and over again, always changing buildings.

WEDDING BELLS

We had been living in Toronto for about a year when the time finally came for Alex to "pop the question." When he asked her, Mom said yes. She was ready to *seal* her new life and turn a new page from which to start fresh. They were married on October 4, 1969.

The ceremony was performed in a little church; in attendance were the three of us and two witnesses who were Mom's friends, although I didn't remember them.

After the wedding, I recall Mom standing on the church steps just outside the door. She leaned over and whispered in my ear, "I don't really love him. I'm just marrying him because you need a father." She could be quite blunt at times.

Settling in was hard and I wasn't sure where I fitted in. As managers of huge building complexes our home life was less than normal. And there didn't seem to be any kids around for me to play with.

People would be at our door all hours of the day and night with crazy issues like water leaks or lockouts. They had a wide variety of other complaints, too. And then there were rent collections, new renter prospects, constant maintenance, and clean up. It was all so disruptive.

We were employed at four separate properties over a three-year period and each time we changed buildings I had to change schools. I was always the "new kid" so I was always on the outside looking in.

Being a loner became very natural for me. I found it easier to be anti-social and on my own rather than to try making new friends all the time. It just worked better.

FRIGHTENED

One day, I was walking across the schoolyard on my way home. As I reached the fence I was met by some people in a big black car. It seemed like they wanted me to get in. I wasn't sure, but my gut feeling, even for a nine-year-old, was bad. I was afraid something dreadful would happen.

So, I slowly turned and backed my way across the grass and returned to the school. I asked someone to call my mom so that my parents could come to get me.

By this time my mother had legal custody of me but she was still afraid my father may have sent someone to the school to steal me away. I knew I was my mother's treasure. I was her only child, and she suffered to keep me with her.

She walked away from a marriage gone bad, and in the divorce settlement, she voluntarily gave up all financial support including alimony just so she could have me. I was all she wanted and she said she was darned if she was going to lose me now.

FAR, FAR AWAY

I don't think my father even knew where we were. But because of that incident, my mother was convinced that Dad was after me so she insisted that Alex make arrangements for us to move far, far away. He agreed. I don't recall speaking to Dad after the divorce until I turned 18.

We packed up everything, putting most of our belongings into a crate that we shipped ahead of us, by train. That left us with just a few personal effects to travel with, so we hopped in our car and headed west; almost as far west as one could go. Those were big steps for our little family.

Alex, whom I was calling "Dad" did not want to drive straight across Canada "as the crow flies." The reason? I don't know. Maybe he wanted more adventure.

So, with our big car packed, we crossed over into the United States and journeyed first South, then East, then West, and then North, crisscrossing back and forth over the entire country for the next thirty days. It was grand!

As we journeyed along like vagabonds our trip probably turned into three times the length it could have been. For me, it was great fun seeing the sights, staying in motels, and dining at some of the finest restaurants, ever, like Howard Johnson's. I liked stopping there because they offered 28 flavors of ice cream.

And then there were other times when we parked on the side of the road, ate spam sandwiches, and slept in the car. A month is a long time for a kid. Sometimes I wondered if we'd ever get there, wherever "there" was.

CHAPTER FIVE

DONUTS AND POSTCARDS

There were so many experiences worth mentioning. Let me share a few. I remember our stay-over in San Francisco. We had slept in the car the night before, on one of the city streets, and in the morning, my dad and I awoke first and then my mom began to stir.

Dad said he wanted to go out for breakfast but *she* wanted to stay behind and fiddle with her hair. So we left her and ventured down the street to a local diner. There, we feasted on an array of yummy donuts. It was the best breakfast, ever.

Our trip included many cities and historical landmarks like the Empire State Building, the Liberty Bell, the Chesapeake Bay Bridge, the mansions of Rhode Island, the St. Louis Arch, the beautiful Gulf Coast shores, the California Redwoods, the Golden Gate Bridge and the famous gambling town of Reno, Nevada just to name a few. Remember, I was just a kid from Canada.

At nearly every stop we made, if there were postcards handy I would ask for some. I had picture postcards of the Washington Monument in Washington D.C., Mount McKinley the tallest mountain in North America, Mammoth Cave National Park in Kentucky, the river-boats on the Mississippi river, famous places in New Orleans, Chimney Rock in Nebraska, the Liberty Bell, lighthouses on the shores of the oceans, and so much more.

By the end of the trip, I had so many postcards that I had to keep them in a two-gallon box. That box became my prized possession and my invisible friend.

I loved going through and revisiting the dozens of places we'd been; it was like a magical wonderland in which to reminisce. By holding those cards in my hands and seeing the pictures, they stirred up marvelous memories of a young child who was able to enjoy fantastic things.

Had we never made that trip I would have missed out on so much. I treasured that box over the years. Now, though the postcards and the donuts are gone, the adventures have been forever carved in my mind. At least I can think back on it every so often.

FORTY-NINE HUNDRED KILOMETERS

Eventually, we ended up in the north-western part of Canada landing in a little town called Terrace, British Columbia, (B.C.) with a population of about nine or ten thousand people. I was going on ten years old.

By this time I was missing my real dad but finally, Mom was pretty sure he didn't know where we were so I had to accept the possibility that I may never see him again. Or would I?

Well, anyway, Mom felt sure there was no chance he could steal me from way up here. Now, it was up to me to live *this* life at *this* moment, whatever that meant, even though it was all controlled by the adults. All I could do was go along for the ride. So I put everything out of my mind and focused on the present: a new school, and maybe some new friends.

Terrace is a town located about 100 miles from the Pacific Ocean and is lodged right next to the Skeena River. It is surrounded by beautiful high mountains which are snow-capped all year long. The bad thing is that Terrace gets a combined amount of ten or twelve feet of snow every year, on average.

The Kitselas and Kitsumkalum people are tribes of the Tsimshian Nation and there's archeological evidence that they have lived in the Terrace area for a few millenniums. Terrace is one of the oldest, continuously occupied regions of the world.

Was it much different than being in Montreal? Oh, yes! And the 4,900 kilometers, or 3,050 miles, away from what I had known all my life seemed a million miles away.

Everything familiar to me had changed and now I was starting over. Since I had become so used to turmoil and change in my young life, I was prepared to turn over a new leaf once again and looked forward to new and exciting adventures.

THE PLIGHT OF THE SONGBIRD

I continued to grow in my God-given love of music. Day by day and song by song I was more deeply attracted to it than ever and hoped to participate in it one day, soon.

Every song I heard on the radio, every songbird in the trees, and even the majestic beauty of the mountains around me all became marvelous companions. In that pursuit, I found friendship in rhythms and notes and all kinds of instrumental sounds.

In some way, I think I understood how a little unborn bird must feel as it pecks its way out of a shell knowing there's something out there, believing that's what it was meant to do; that's why it was created.

Maybe I was like the snowbird in the song, *Snowbird*, sung by Anne Murray. I knew there was a nest I was supposed to occupy and that nest was *music.*

Just as surely as the snowbird would one day be free, I was determined to find my way out of my shell, too, no matter how hard I had to peck away at the poverty and loneliness confining my life.

29

Maybe then, I'd stretch my wings and fly into the wonderful world I longed for, as the artist God created me to be.

IF ONLY I COULD FLY

It was either May or June of 1970 when the song, *Snowbird* came out. It was a big, worldwide success. Not only did Anne Murray have her first hit but she also received a gold record, the first ever won by a Canadian female artist. She was very popular and to my surprise, she was only 15 years older than me.

When she started she was turned down by a certain record company but two years later the same producer gave her another chance and she started recording. She was young but her dreams came true. Would I have a chance, too?

The words to *Snowbird* in some ways tell my heart's story: a young aspiring musician trying to get away from a place of heartache, wishing to be like the snowbird, to lift itself up and fly away.

Snowbird
Written by Gene MacLellan

Beneath this snowy mantle cold and clean
The unborn grass lies waiting
for its coat to turn to green
The snowbird sings the song he always sings
And speaks to me of flowers
that will bloom again in spring

When I was young
my heart was young then, too
Anything that it would tell me
that's the thing that I would do

But now I feel such emptiness within
for the thing that I want most in life's
the thing that I can't win

Spread your tiny wings and fly away
And take the snow back with you
where it came from on that day
The one I love forever is untrue
and if I could you know that I would
Fly away with you
Yeah, if I could you know that I would
Fl-y-y-y away with you

A SONG IN MY HEART

I'm not sure songs like that are written anymore
but this one, by Gene MacLellan and beautifully sung
by Anne Murray, takes me back to those awesome
times of my youth when the word "happiness" meant a
lot.

Because of artists like Anne Murray and Simon
and Garfunkel, music would inspire me for the rest of
my life.

At the same time, I didn't realize that before
hope could be fulfilled, there would be pain. Poverty
and lack of opportunity created cruel circumstances
that held me back, but I knew I would never give up. I
knew in my heart I would make it.

A RAINBOW OF MUSIC

Where ever I went I saw and heard music, as it
absorbed my heartbeat and my breath. It became an
unquenchable passion.

I saw music in the street signs, on the billboards,
and in the shadows of the buildings. In everything that
moved I saw a rhythm of patterns that created

melodies in my head. I even heard music in the automobiles going past me down the street.

Beautiful rhythms rolled like thunder from the towering snow-capped mountains, gently brushing by me in the summer breezes. And I was inspired by the raindrops as they wiggled and danced their way down the window pane of our kitchen widow. The rhythm of their sounds penetrated my every waking moment.

While the freezing Canadian temperatures and the deep snows tried to dissuade and discourage me, it wasn't possible because what I had was buried too deeply to be expunged.

Was there a price to pay for this love? Yes. People began to think of me as disconnected and aloof. I lost interest in many things even if it meant chasing my passion to the very end of the musical rainbow.

MY COMFORT/MY PRISON

Socially, I was indeed sort of a recluse. And that was alright, I thought because no matter how tough things got, I always had music to comfort me. But my little world had become like a prison.

I wrestled over questions like, "How could I find a way to play music?" and, "How could I get involved with other players?" and, "How *could* I express how I felt to my parents and others so they would understand what was living inside of me?"

Without an instrument or music books to learn from, and no money to buy them, I was living in a virtual prison of silence.

BUT GOD . . . HOW?

I did peak out from behind my shell, sometimes. For instance, in fifth grade, my school was planning a *fun-night.* They planned a bake sale, a game of musical chairs, refreshments, and a dance at the end of the evening. I decided I wanted to go, on one condition: I would need a new pair of shoes.

I saw a nice pair in one of the stores in town, but they cost eight dollars and my mother didn't have the money to buy them for me. I thought about what else I could do and finally came up with an idea.

Not far from my house was a drive-in movie theater. Next to the parking area was a large ditch or embankment filled with empty soda cans that people threw out of their car windows during shows.

Back then, I could collect one penny for every two soda cans. So, I ambitiously hauled 1600 cans in two, old-fashioned metal buckets, each holding 21 cans. I don't know how many hours or trips it took but a few days later, I called the recycle company. They picked up my 1600 pieces of aluminum and gave me my eight dollars, and I bought my shoes.

I attended the event; it came and went. But ever present in my mind was how to get involved in music. I had so many questions; they were like a garland of words hanging over my troubled brow. Yet, I continued to *believe* because something deeper than life itself stirred inside, pushing me, and giving me the strength to hang on.

When I cried, "God, how?" His strong spirit replied, "Your day will come. Just be content for now and have faith."

Time passed and I kept waiting. The winds of hopelessness were like the biting northern winds that whipped against me as I walked to school, feeling trapped in a storm of despair.

As much as I needed to protect myself with a warm coat and scarf, I also needed to wrap myself in *hope* to soften the agony in my heart. I agonized over my struggles; they mounted into a losing battle. I was hopelessly hoping . . . for *hope*.

33

CHAPTER SIX

ONE DOOR OPENS; ANOTHER DOOR SHUTS

I believe God was on my side because only He could have solved my problems.

First, while I didn't yet have a "relationship" with God, I felt "led" to change schools. I know it was the Lord, working in my life, even then.

I started at Clarence Michael Elementary in grade five but I didn't like it there. No reason, really . . . but I was moved to ask if I could switch schools.

The school board was against it because the other school wasn't in my district. Finally, they agreed, so I attended Cassie Hall Elementary instead.

Second, after I started grade six, I heard the school was offering a music class. I was excited to sign up but I was facing an obstacle. I needed an instrument to make it through the door; the door to my dreams.

My situation seemed impossible. It was like the door that just opened, shut. I knew without an instrument the reality of that class was short-lived. How could life be so cruel? I was so close and yet so far.

All I knew was Mom and Dad struggled to keep us clothed, fed, and housed. Even then, we sometimes hardly had enough to eat. But, should I also starve my music-hungry soul? Is this how it was? It didn't make any sense.

I asked my mother for a guitar but just as I figured, she said she didn't have the money. So, that was out of the question. Then I started looking at ukuleles. There was one displayed in the local music shop in town. It was eleven dollars.

Even in 1969-70 that wasn't a great deal of money but it was more than my mom could spare. I went back to her again and again--in tears--but she kept saying no; she couldn't do it.

After crying my eyes out I reluctantly thought I'd have to give up. But . . . it was a "must-have" for me. It was a matter of life and death. Right?

THE MIRACLE

Then it happened. Miraculously, from some unknown source, Mom managed to scrape up the funds for my "store-window-instrument." Wow. It was amazing and grand. I cried.

When we went to the music store my heart was in my throat. The ukulele was still there in the window. I stared at it. I thought it was beautiful. I could hardly stand still.

Mom walked to the counter and told the salesperson she wanted the item in the storefront. My stomach fluttered and my legs could hardly hold me as he walked to the ledge, brought it back, and handed it to me.

The first time I touched it, a string cried out, "I'm yours . . . we will be wonderful together."

Chills ran from my fingertips to the bottom of my feet. I couldn't believe it as I walked out with my own ukulele in its little cardboard box. I tucked it safely under my arm and cradled it like it was alive; it was going to become my very best friend.

Finally, those feelings buried deep within me would be set free. I loved it! Now, at last, I could begin to talk in a language I understood.

A TIME TO LEARN

Once home, I unpacked the instrument and the little instruction book that came with it and I went straight to my room. I began the work of practicing and each day I progressed through the pages until I learned enough chords to play a few songs. In three weeks, I knew enough to participate in the class.

The class met twice a week for an hour. We would play and sing one song after another for the whole sixty minutes. It was heavenly. I was the luckiest girl that ever lived.

My wishes had come true and I was grateful to my mother who worked this miracle for me. I was riding a rainbow to heaven and though I didn't realize it, God was also shaping my destiny.

A couple of years later I found a cheap guitar. I saved up for a long time to buy it and learned to play it, too. With it, God opened new horizons I had only dared to dream about.

As an eleven-year-old in sixth grade, I had already been in several schools since leaving Montreal. My dad, Alex, had us jumping from one place to another but I wanted our rambling to stop. It was fun but I didn't want to give up what I now had. *Here* is where I wanted to stay.

MUSIC CLASS: MY PROVING GROUND

Two teachers headed up my music class, Mr. Orr and Mr. Goss. They both played guitar and taught students to play guitar and ukulele. They had also transcribed all the popular songs of the day, writing out the lyrics and the chords on big paper charts.

I remember songs like *Trailers For Sale or Rent, Killing Me Softly, Snow Bird, Leaving On a Jet Plane,* and even *The Canadian Railroad Trilogy* which was about 20 minutes long.

For me, getting into that class with those two great teachers was like a lost person finding a roadmap home. That marvelous class inspired me to play and write my own songs. That's when I wrote my first song called, *The Seasons*.

In my alone times, whether I was at home or at school, I worked on that song, trying to get every part of it just right. I couldn't write out the musical notes, so I simply wrote out "rows of dashes" to indicate where the melody went up or down.

When I felt it was ready I wanted to show it to Mr. Goss, but because I was so shy I had to fight with myself to find the courage.

Eventually, I approached Mr. Goss in tears one day and handed him a piece of paper with little lines all over it. I explained that it was a song I had written and he said,

"Can you sing it for me?"

"No," I said, "I can't do that."

His answer was very soft: "Well how can I know how it goes if you don't sing it?" My feet felt like they were riveted to the floor. But I did recognize the calm and encouraging way he spoke.

I couldn't answer him but after some coaxing, he led me to the piano and said, "If you will sing just a few notes at a time, I will find the notes on the piano and write them down on special music paper. So I agreed.

Mr. Goss listened carefully, noting the melody of the verses and the chorus as he wrote out the song on his own hand-drawn staff paper; I still have that paper in my possession. Finally, he played my song from his notes.

Did he laugh at me or ridicule me or tell me to go away? No. He was very supportive and listened attentively like he truly cared. To my surprise, he was so impressed that he decided to send it to the famous Canadian singer, Anne Murray.

Her response was very gracious. She sent me a nice letter back saying that although she couldn't use my song just then, she liked it.

The attention and help from Mr. Goss as well as the answer from Anne Murray gave me a little more confidence. I think God was showing me He had given me a gift that would be with me forever.

MY WINGS

But the story doesn't end there. When the school year came to a close, Mr. Goss decided to teach my song to our school choir so we could perform it at our year-end concert in front of all the parents.

It was amazing. I was hearing *my* song; every note and every word that came from inside of me. And God blessed me even more when Mr. Goss asked me to sing a couple of solo parts. What a thrill that was for this shy, eleven-year-old, Szúnyog.

Mr. Goss was so kind to have worked with me. *My* musical creation was performed there at Cassie Hall Elementary. Were my musical wings beginning to show? Maybe so. Maybe they were even blossoming and soon I would fly away to that magical place I loved so much.

THE SEASONS
By Kathy Debreceni

VERSES:
1. So sparkly is the water, running down the stream
Spring, Spring...
When all the snow has gone
So beautiful the birds all singing in the greens
My wait for Spring is much too long

2. So beautiful the birds all singing in the trees
Summer...
See the colt trot by,
and the flowers in the garden, dressed so prettily
Summer went too fast, oh why?

3.See the leaves a-hurling in the breeze
Fall...
It leaves the branches so bare
We're all getting ready for the winter's freeze
But still the weather is quite fair

4.See the snow a-trickling down
Winter...
The ground is covered with snow
Not a soul will roam in town
I wish that all of this would go

CHORUS:
Spring is happy and gay
Summer is cheerfully bright
But fall is when the leaves change tune
And you freeze the winter's nights

THE OLD LUMBERMILL ROAD

Another year passed. I was about to turn twelve.
That year we rented a house secluded far back on an
old dirt road near a lumber mill. It was a small, one-
bedroom place so Dad turned the back porch into a
bedroom for me. Even though there were cracks and
holes allowing air to pass through freely, it wasn't too
bad. At least not in the summer.

The downside was during those winter nights, we
sometimes had no heat. We could barely afford to pay
the rent so at times there was not enough money left
over for heating oil, too.

Then, when the Canadian winter winds began to blow and find their way through those crevices in the walls, it became impossible to enjoy my little porch/bedroom.

How did we manage during those times? We dressed in coats and hats and covered up with whatever we could find to stay warm while we slept.

Mom made it all fun. She had a good sense of humor and kept things light-hearted, but still, it wasn't easy. Sometimes we felt like we were going to freeze to death. But we survived.

THE SHAME OF POVERTY

Having enough food was another problem. To get us fed, Dad would, on occasion, come home with food stuffed in his coat pockets and pants that he had stolen from a grocery store. We were ashamed of that but we were hungry, so we ate it with thankfulness

Poverty is a harsh taskmaster. Sometimes the brutal strength of hunger will overtake a person's morals. Even though we *knew* the difference between right and wrong, we looked forward to Dad bringing home that food. The hard lessons we learn are not easily forgotten. Therefore, we should all be kind to one another because we can't often see the battles others are facing.

Our landlord, like many other folks around there, was of an older local Native-Indian heritage. We spent a lot of time with him and his wife watching television. (We didn't have one.) As we all sat together in their living room we shared laughs and treats.

God was so good to use those kind-hearted folks to share their food, their comfort, and their lives with our family. Unfortunately, things were about to change for the worse.

CHAPTER SEVEN

DEATH AT THE DOOR

Because Dad couldn't find steady work he would pick up odd maintenance jobs or anything else he could find to make a couple of dollars. But eventually, he started getting sick. I guess the pressures of trying to support us caused an ulcer to develop in his stomach which grew to the size of a grapefruit.

He ended up in the hospital where doctors gave him about three weeks to live. There, we met a married couple named Bob and Shirley who were staff nurses and were the ones who cared for him through his illness.

The doctors didn't give Dad much hope, but Bob and Shirley came to his room every day and prayed for him. Who knew what effect their prayers would have? We didn't, but Bob and Shirley had faith in a mighty, healing God.

CHRISTIAN FRIENDS

After Dad's ulcer was removed, he began to heal. Yes, Bob and His wife Shirley became very precious to us and we later came to believe God *did* answer their prayers, and ours, allowing my dad to live, so he was around for quite a few more years. (He lived to the age of 94.)

After Dad left the hospital, Bob and Shirley invited us to their church, under Pastor Munroe, and we visited there several times. One Sunday, Mom and Dad both went to the altar and asked Jesus to forgive them of their sins and come into their hearts. They became born-again Christians that day.

Things were still financially hard but the church folks reached out with baskets of food and support.

We developed lifelong friendships that surpassed time and distance. That's how *true* Christians treat each other; we were so thankful for them.

ACCEPTED IN THE BELOVED

Sometime during the summer months after my thirteenth birthday, we were invited to the Pastor's house on a Sunday for a fellowship meal. That's when the Pastor's wife took me into a back bedroom and shared Jesus with me.

I learned that Jesus is a *personal* God, that He loves us and wants to know us, and wants us to know Him. All those who belong to Him are "accepted in the beloved;" that is, we are accepted by God.

She told me how He would stay with me the rest of my life through thick and thin if I would ask Him to come into my heart and be the Lord of my life.

She told me how He would forgive me of anything I had ever done wrong and treat me as If I were His daughter and He would be a loving Father to me.

That's the love I had been looking for. That's the love I so badly needed. It warmed my heart to know I would have the love of a Father who would never abandon me.

So, at the age of 13, I accepted Christ. Years later I found a verse in the Bible, in the first book of Ephesians that says, ***"To the praise of the glory of his grace, wherein he hath made us accepted in the beloved,"*** (Ephesians 1:6; KJV). I knew this was for me.

Later, I joined the youth group and enjoyed singing choruses with them and accompanying them with my guitar. At some point, Pastor Munroe baptized me and Mom together and my parents gave me a brand new, King James Bible which I still own. It goes to church with me every Sunday. Thanks so much, Mom and Dad.

I believe I was truly saved because I had accepted Christ as my Savior and had tasted the goodness of the Lord, Jesus Christ. I never wanted to lose that, even though in my heart I was still a troubled little girl with lots of painful confusion.

I do wish I would have realized how much I needed *inner healing* at the time and that God could make me *whole* . . . if only I had let Him.

MOVING AGAIN

My dad recovered from his surgery but my parents were still facing the same problem: there was no work. They realized we needed to move, but where? Moving to a big city held much more promise for job opportunities, so that year, we left Terrace, and headed to Edmonton, Alberta, about 930 miles away.

I'm not sure why they picked Edmonton. They could have stayed in the province and moved South to Vancouver. But for now, Edmonton seemed as good a choice as any. Though Dad did find work, it took us a while to get on our feet and it was hard going forward as I entered grade seven. The road ahead was cloudy.

BOXES ON TOP OF BOXES

We hoped things would work out but Edmonton didn't deliver on its promise. For some reason, my dad still couldn't find a *decent* job; just temporary, get-by work. So we remained poor and needy and had to go on welfare. We just couldn't make it to the finish line.

For example, we had rented a townhouse but we couldn't furnish it. New furniture was too expensive for us to buy and thrift stores were not abundant back then. The Welfare Department was willing to supply a kitchen table and a mattress for my parents but I was out of luck so Mom bought me a blowup rubber boat to sleep on.

That took care of laying down to sleep but what about our clothes? Where would we put it all? We couldn't afford dressers and no matter how hard we looked we couldn't find any for free. There was one solution: we used cardboard boxes.

Stacked one on top of another, the boxes made a kind of open-faced dresser to store stuff. There were no drawers, but we still had an organized place for our things and it was better than just having piles on the floor. At least I didn't feel like we were bums, nesting in an alley or living out of a car, which we had done before.

CHURCH LIFE

One of my best memories during that period was when my Mother and I visited a Pentecostal church. It was amazing because I could *feel* the Spirit of God. He was *alive* there, in a way I hadn't experienced before.

All the young people would stand and praise God with their hands in the air in a real attitude of awe. It was powerful and unknown to me. I discovered a new feeling of God's special presence. There's an expression that says, "as the praises go up, blessings come down."

But those were *my* feelings, not Mom's. It was clear to me that she didn't like the services. She was afraid of what was going on. She sort of *yanked* me out of there and we never went back. I'm sure if I had stayed I would have been filled with the Holy Spirit.

We instead began attending Beulah Alliance Church. We enjoyed it there as a family and went quite regularly for several months. Eventually, we drifted away from that, too.

All the while, I was greatly influenced by the peer pressure at school which was very strong. Why was that? Because I desperately wanted to "fit in."

So, when kids offered me cigarettes, you guessed it, I started smoking. It helped me feel like I was part of the "in" crowd and I badly needed that. I didn't want to be an "outsider" anymore. Later on, I'll tell you how I managed to quit smoking . . . it's a remarkable story.

DREAM, DREAM, DREAM

Here we go again with the pattern I was used to: I entered yet another new school. This time it was Strathern Junior High, for seventh grade. One after another, the names of schools I attended were becoming a blur behind me. At least this school would make me happy, for a time. Here's why:

I hardly finished getting enrolled when I heard some exciting news. I welcomed it like pretty, rolling ocean waves. This school had a band program! Oh, yeah! I needed to find out more about *that.*

All I could think of was learning a musical instrument. Could it really be or would disappointment come again? I hoped God would help me like He had at Cassie Hall.

HERE, TRY THIS ONE

I found out where I could sign up but I didn't know what instrument to try, so I tried several different ones.

I started with the flute and I stuck with it for about six months but I didn't like it. It made me dizzy to have to take such deep breaths to play it.

I switched to trombone, mostly because I could create that age-old trombone sound when you blow into it and move the slide all the way down and back up again. But still, this wasn't the instrument for me.

From that I switched over to the tuba, then the sousaphone, then the clarinet, and finally--whether they were getting tired of me, I didn't know--they put a drum in front of me. And that was *it.*

I gravitated to that snare drum like a hungry dog after a juicy bone. I was happy. Anxious. And willing to work at it, no matter what. Playing the drums is what I felt I was born to do. I didn't know it yet, but God had an amazing future planned. Yes, I was a happy camper.

AGAIN?

At some point, my parents decided to move from Edmonton back to Terrace and my heart was broken. I was sad to have to leave behind everything I had fallen in love with: Strathern and the music program. And besides that, I was so tired of moving. It made me depressed.

I don't know why they wanted to move but I can only guess it was because they missed their friends in Terrace. It might have also been important for them because Dad wasn't having much luck finding a good job that he liked. "What about me?" I thought. "Didn't I count?"

I guess they figured we had nothing to lose, so in June, when school was over, we left for Terrace. We left everything behind and hit the road. We were always moving and always losing something in the process.

At fourteen years of age, I was old enough to see that I wanted a better life. I needed more structure and security, and I was tired of packing up what I could while abandoning the rest. I wished things would have been different.

Every year I was enrolling in a new school. Sometimes it was more than one school per year. I went to a total of fifteen schools in twelve years. How I managed to get an education, I'll never know.

I always passed everything even though I didn't pay attention in class. Maybe God was still with me; I hoped so because I was going to need Him as the next part of my life was about to unfold.

CHAPTER EIGHT

THE ROOT OF ALL EVIL

After we moved back to Terrace, Dad continued to work here and there. Eventually, he found a permanent job as a hotel desk clerk, working from midnight until early morning. He was there for a few months when something went terribly wrong.

You see, we had been poor for so long and needed money so badly that Dad became enticed by the amount of cash he was handling every night. I'm sure it was a tremendous temptation because one night the lure of money, (the root of all evil), was just too strong, so Dad took all the cash from the drawer and ran.

He hopped into our car and drove away, never looking back, leaving all thought of us behind. The authorities found him about a week later in Calgary, Alberta, over 800 miles away, where they arrested him. He was tried and convicted and he was sentenced to almost a year in prison.

With Dad's income gone, Mom and I had to go back on Welfare. We moved into a one-room apartment that used to be a motel. We were quite down and out. The days were filled with scouring the thrift stores for clothes and household items and humbly receiving handouts.

Mom would write to my dad every day and he sent as many letters back. When we weren't writing letters, Mom and I would watch soap operas on TV after school. Either that or I'd spend time practicing my guitar. I had learned a lot of chords and had many songs piled up in a binder that I would sing over and over again.

BANG THE TRASH CAN

While that was going on, there *was* a bright spot. I was just starting ninth grade and was informed that my school had both a concert band and a marching band program.

Since I had already been playing the snare drum the year before, I was able to join up as a percussionist. I played snare drum, bass drum, triangle, tambourine, and many other percussion instruments you might think of as "gadgets." It was such fun.

I'll explain it this way: a percussionist plays individual instruments such as those mentioned plus bells, xylophone, wood blocks, claves, timpani which are commonly called kettle drums, and anything you can beat with a stick. And I do mean anything! I've even seen trash can lids utilized.

In contrast to being a "percussionist," anyone who just "plays the drums" is called a "drummer;" they play the drum set; that's it. At this point, I was called a percussionist and I couldn't get enough of it.

A TRIP TO THE U.S.

In 1974, our marching band got to travel to the United States, to Spokane, Washington to perform at the Worlds Fair. Part of that trip was by bus, and part of it was on a ferry boat that went from Prince Rupert, BC to Vancouver, BC.

The boat ride lasted through the night hours and I was sicker than a dog the whole time. I have suffered from motion sickness since the age of two and I don't travel by car very well, nor can I even go on a park swing. For sure I couldn't manage the rocking motion of a boat in the water. But here I was on a large ferry, and I was turning every shade of green there was.

It was all worth it though because I desperately wanted to be part of this band and play music at the World Fair. It was special and I--lil' ole' me--felt like I was accomplishing something great. So, I endured and aside from the seasickness, I enjoyed my trip with the band. I'll never forget it.

THE BAND ROOM

I used to linger around in the band room during lunch and after school. They did something they called "jamming." This was all new but I wanted to learn everything I could so I started hanging out there.

One day some guys started playing, *Joy to the World*. You know the song. It starts with, "Jeremiah was a bullfrog." When I heard the song, of course, I knew it because I had heard it on the radio plenty of times.

I jumped on the drum set for the very first time and just started playing. I didn't have to figure it out. I just played and soared along with the other players. *That* was incredible.

How was this possible? Well, I had made friends with a guy in our neighborhood who was one of the local natives. My mom and his mom were friends and that's how I got to know her son, Neil.

We used to sit in his room at his parents' house spinning records for hours on end. One of the bands I discovered through him was Creedence Clearwater Revival, (CCR). I fell in love with that band. The neatest thing about their music was how clearly I could hear the drums. The beat stood out and was very easy to pick up.

While listening, I worked out all the various parts of the drum set, slapping my hands on my knees and tapping my feet on the floor to the rhythm.

In the band room when the boys started playing the bullfrog song, I found I could instantly play. That was an absolute thrill. From then on I simply assumed that the drums were made for me and they'd be mine until the end of time.

At the end of that school year, the concert band performed a concert. One of the songs we played was, "Jesus Christ Superstar." I begged the band director to let me play the drum set for that song and he agreed.

On the evening of the concert, I got to perform in front of everyone. Included in the song was a *four-bar drum solo* which I got to play.

I'll always remember how the air stood still when we came to that part. It wasn't a "Phil Collins" moment, (although I've had the pleasure of hearing the song, *In the Air Tonight*, at a live, Phil Collins, concert).

My solo was like an eternity captured inside of a moment, and that's where I wanted to stay.

I experienced a new birth and I could see my future. In fact, I used to babysit a couple of children so I could earn a little extra money, and one night while being driven home, the Father asked me, "What do you want to be when you grow up?" Without hesitation, I said, "a drummer." I had no doubt. This is what I was meant to do.

PASTOR, YOU'RE WRONG!

A major downfall was headed my way but I didn't see it coming. It would take me the *next twelve years* to reverse this wrong turn in my life.

The devil is a foul, sneaky creature and sometimes he tempts us with *good* things that eventually move us away from the Lord. He attempts to sway us by appealing to our desires and our sense of logic.

51

Logic is a good thing, but God will defy what sometimes seems logical because His plans are higher than our plans. We can't see around the corners but he can see the end from the beginning. If we would only trust Him, our lives would add up to so much more than they do.

By the age of fourteen, I had developed quite a taste for rock and roll music including Heavy Metal. One of my favorite bands was Black Sabbath. I nearly wore out their album, *Master of Reality*.

I had no idea what they were singing about; I couldn't understand their diction. I missed a lot of lyrics because I was so focused on the instruments. The powerful sounds of the edgy guitar and the drums were so solid that to me it was all very cool.

My Pastor at church didn't think it was cool at all. He took a hard stand against the modern music of the day. He told us--the young people in the church--if we wanted to be followers of Christ, we needed to stop listening to that rubbish and burn all of our records and throw them away.

What?! That was a horrible idea. There was *no way* I was going to destroy my albums. I lived and breathed that stuff. That music was "who I am." No, sorry to say, that wasn't going to fly.

RELEASED FROM PRISON

While all that was going on, my dad's sentence was coming to an end. He was released from prison in the spring of that year, so once again--you guessed it--my family packed whatever we could fit into our car and moved back to Edmonton.

The reason for this move was to separate us from the embarrassment of my dad's prison time. Also, he still needed a good job and wanted to try the big city one more time. If we didn't move, our living situation would continue to be dismal. So, out of necessity, we found ourselves back in Alberta. Maybe this time it would be better.

That Fall I was going into tenth grade and I was going to start a new school so, I'd be "the new kid" once again. And this is where I *sealed* that wrong turn in my life. I made a terrible decision that would drag me down for years to come.

CHAPTER NINE

DISILLUSIONED

When we first moved back to Edmonton, we lived downtown in a boarding house. Several people lived there and we had a couple of rooms upstairs while sharing the kitchen and bathroom with others. It was clumsy but it was enough to get us by.

I had already been dabbling in alcohol and cigarettes. Along with that, I was still haunted by my Pastor's reprimands over the evils of rock music. And that's where I drew the line, so to speak. I not only loved music but it gave me a new position in life--one this poor kid hadn't had before. It gave me a sense of self-esteem; something I desperately needed.

I was becoming disillusioned with Christianity *as I understood it.*

I always felt like the girl who *had* nothing, who *was* nothing and would *be* nothing, but this God-given gift of mine caused people to admire me because of my talent. I needed to be accepted and that acceptance through music was something I couldn't give up no matter what the Pastor said.

I needed music like other people need air to breathe. The Pastor just didn't understand.

THE TRUTH

What I didn't know was that God wanted me to *walk* with Him and to know that *He* was the one who put music into my life and my heart. *He* was the one who made all these lovely sights and sounds possible. But at the same time, He wanted my fellowship. He didn't want me to give *Him* up.

I wish I could have understood God's truths back then. It would have saved me from many heartaches.

But being blinded by worldly things, I had no idea of the magnitude of what I was about to do.

Abandoning God was a sure step into a life of rebellion filled with danger and discouragement for a long time to come. How I wish I had never changed course but I did not understand God's truths . . .

Consider the following old sayings:
1 *"The truth will set you free, but first, it will make you miserable."* (Yes, it's hard to be confronted with the truth.)
2 *"Lies get people into trouble, but honesty is its own defense."* (Honesty is the best policy.)
3 *"Truth is truth no matter how it's told, even if it's an embarrassment to the teller."* (It may hurt to speak the truth but it's the best thing to do.)

Here's what happened to me, exactly the way it unfolded. I *did* experience these things so please don't glibly dismiss my words.

THE PRICE OF REBELLION

One night in my room at the boardinghouse, I decided to pray to God for the last time. That's right, the last time. I decided that my parents were wrong, the preacher was wrong, and God was wrong, but I was right and only my music was right for me.

I said, *"Dear God, I can't follow You anymore because You want to take my music away from me. I just can't understand why You would give me such a wonderful gift and then want to take it back.*

"So now, because I love it, and because it makes me feel accepted by others, I can't live without it.

"Maybe You mean well but I just don't see what's wrong with what I'm doing. Following You is like trying to keep a bunch of rules that I can't manage to live with.

"I'm sorry but I just can't do it anymore. So as of now, I'm going to have to say goodbye to You . . .

Amen."

And that's where I left it.

Almost immediately, I saw evidence of demons entering my room. My guitar had been carefully propped against the wall but suddenly it started to play by itself. Fearfully I began to look all around.

As I looked out the window I saw an ugly face staring back at me through the glass. It had long black hair and a marred face; it was very frightening, especially to a young fifteen-year-old girl who had not been a Christian very long.

I sat straight up in my bed and at that very moment, the door to my bedroom began to open. I clutched my blanket in fear and waited for what was coming next, but nothing happened.

Finally, I dared to get out of bed and tip-toe to the still partially open door. I looked down the hall to see if someone was there but the house was quiet. I didn't know what else to do so I shut my door and went back to bed because I felt safer under the covers.

I didn't know my bed covers couldn't protect me. God was my keeper and He would still look out for me even though I had turned my back on Him. He still had His hand of love upon me, even when I thought I could walk away and face life on my own. But I would have to pay a price for my rebellion.

I will never forget that night; neither will God.

STARTING OVER AGAIN IN EDMONTON

Eventually, that frightful night became a faded memory. Time erased it from my mind. Now I was just looking ahead to figure out what *I* could accomplish.

We didn't live in the rooming house for long. We found an apartment close to my high school; in fact, it was just across the street. We moved in at the end of the summer and I was looking forward to school in the Fall.

I was always looking for ways to earn a little extra money and found a couple of babysitting jobs. I met a lady in our building that had me over to babysit from time to time. They had a two-year-old son that needed care when she and her husband went out.

I remember that the child had a great big yellow teddy bear that sat in the living room. I guess I was still quite a child myself because I let that "what if" curiosity get the better of me.

One night while I was babysitting, I was looking at it and I wondered what would happen if I lit a match and held the flame real close to the fur. Well, I got my answer.

My heart was beating out of my chest but I just couldn't help myself as I lit the match and held it next to that pretty golden material. I knew it was wrong but I continued anyway.

In a second or two, the flame flashed across the surface and it singed the whole back side of the bear. I tried to clip off the burnt fibers to hide the fact that they had been scorched. Good grief! How was I going to get out of this mess?

I don't remember ever getting in trouble over it but I'm sure they noticed it. To this day I don't know how I could do something so dumb and so wrong. I could have burned the building down. It was time for me to grow up!

Yes, God was still taking care of me. Does that mean it's alright to tell God you're walking away from Him and never suffer the consequences? Not at all. It's just that *He* is faithful even when *we* aren't.

The Bible says God loves us with an everlasting love and I'm sure glad He does. His love protected me that night just as He did many other times, even when I wasn't aware of it.

PHYLLIS

There was another lady in our building. Her name was Phyllis Shandro. She lived with a tremendous handicap. She had a brittle bone disease and when she wasn't in bed she was in a wheelchair; those were her only two places to be.

The disease stunted her growth never allowing her to grow beyond about four feet in height. Her bones were very susceptible to breakage so she had to keep her legs in removable casts at all times.

She had caregivers during the week but needed someone on the weekends, so as a fifteen-year-old I would stay with her overnight and would carry her to the bathroom as needed. I would also cook and clean for her (as best as I could) and bathe her and wash her hair.

She was quite an outgoing person and she really liked to laugh, so of course, we had some fun times together. Often, I would get her dressed, put her into her wheelchair, and take her places. We'd even go "drinking." Yes, I took her to the bars. I was way under age but they would let me come in because I was her helper.

WAIT! GO BACK!

I remember one time when we were at the mall; it must have been a Friday afternoon because the bank was very busy that day. She had to withdraw some money but the bank teller lines were extra long.

After waiting in line for a while, I noticed that people were staring at Phyllis. She was rather deformed and was quite a spectacle for some folks, I guess.

Well, it upset me. Finally, I couldn't take it anymore and I spun her chair around and took off with her down through the shopping center.

Phyllis was laughing and hollering, "Wait! Go back . . . I still have to do my banking!"

I don't remember if we went back or not. But I explained to her how I felt and how I wanted to protect her. She understood. She was used to it, and it didn't bother her. Phyllis was a good person.

All the while I was helping Phyllis she was helping me. She taught me a lot of domestic skills. And while I was already quite good at being organized, she heightened those talents even more.

There was one rule she gave me about organizing that I will never forget; I still use it to this day: when you've established a place for certain items to "live," even if it's in a bag, inside a box, on the top shelf of the closet, *always use that spot.*

So if after you've put everything away you find something that goes in one of those places, you must make the effort to go to the closet, reach up to the shelf, open the box, or get the bag out, and put the stray item inside.

Furthermore, if you have to unpack and repack your storage place three times in a row to get everything back into its "place to live," then do it. Don't just lay the item down or shove it onto a shelf somewhere saying "I'll take care of it later." *Always* put it away, right then. If you want to be organized this is good advice.

CHAPTER TEN

MY FIRST SCHOOL DANCE

Now that I was in grade ten the peer pressure was greater than ever. I had already been introduced to alcohol, but I didn't yet understand what the limits were. I figured that if I wanted to get *really* drunk, I would need to drink *a lot of booze.*

My girlfriends from school knew how to bootleg liquor, meaning she could get it even though she wasn't old enough. I was afraid to do it myself but I went with them to get the job done.

We would all sit around outside the liquor store with cash in hand and ask different ones going in if they would buy us a bottle of something. We always found someone who was willing.

The month was October. One day we heard there was going to be a "sock hop" at school. It would be a noon-time dance and they would play *canned* music and offer refreshments. Us girls thought it would be fun to get some liquor and go to my house while my parents were at work, drink the morning away, and then go to the dance.

I wanted to get loaded that day so I got my hands on a 26-ounce bottle of Lamb's Navy rum. I didn't have any mix so I had to use orange juice. It was nasty. Nonetheless, I drank the first half of the bottle with the juice in fifteen minutes. After that, I drank the rest, straight.

It was getting close to noon so we all bundled up and walked over to the school. The dance was in the gym and many students were already on the dance floor, swaying to the music.

I spotted a boy I liked and by golly, at that moment, I had the confidence to slide over next to him, put my arms around him and kiss him on the cheek. He looked into my "goo-goo eyes" as if to say, "*Ewe!*" To my surprise, he politely slinked away from me so I just plopped myself down on the floor and sat there.

The room was spinning fast and I didn't feel so good. I started to lean over like I was going to lie down, but then someone spotted me and tried to prop me back up. It was no use. I was losing consciousness.

A couple more kids came along on either side of me and got me up on my feet. Then we all headed to the nurses' station.

ALMOST IN TROUBLE

I remember being sort of dragged down the hallway. Once I was seated in front of the nurse I could barely respond to her questions. The next thing I know, my parents were walking in the door. From there we all went to the hospital where I stayed all day.

Luckily, they *did not* pump my stomach, so I don't know how they treated me, but I think someone said, "It's just going to have to wear off." I guess I could have died. That was a *lot* of alcohol for a 120-pound girl.

They finally released me around nine o'clock that evening. When I got home I went straight to bed. I was still seeing triple images of everything, so, I just closed my eyes and drifted off.

The next day my parents asked me what happened. I just told them I was unwittingly "drugged." They bought it, and that was the end of it. Well, my mom bought the story for sure. My dad, not so much. I could tell by the way he looked at me that he didn't believe me. But he never said a word.

ANOTHER SCHOOL DANCE

Up until now, I had never had a serious boyfriend. I found that boys didn't pay much attention to me. I never felt very pretty, so maybe my lack of confidence overwhelmed my personality more than my lack of looks.

I remember going to a school dance one Friday night. I don't know if I met up with friends there or not but I do remember that I had drunk a fair amount of liquor before showing up. (I assure you though, it wasn't near 26 ounces.)

My biggest reason for going at all was because there was a live band at the event. When I walked into the gymnasium things were well underway. The sound of hard rock music accosted me at the doors.

I found a blank wall to lean up against and from there I listened. The gym was dimly lit so you couldn't see the other students very well. I remember dancing with a few boys here and there, but I was kind of "out of it" and much of it was a blur.

When the band stopped to take a break, I walked up to one of the players standing near the edge of the stage and said,

"Do you mind if I play your drums?"

He looked at me for a moment and simply said, "Okay."

So I climbed up onto the platform and sat down on the kit. I grabbed the sticks that were laying on the floor-tom. They were big and fat; probably a size 2B. I picked them up and started playing a rock beat. The whole room went silent and turned to stare at me.

I played about a five-minute solo and then I petered out. The audience began to clap and cheer as I staggered off the stage. I was drunk for sure, otherwise, I wouldn't have had the guts to do what I had done.

Now, I was looking for a soft place to fall. And there, standing at the edge of the stage, was a nice-looking young man with arms outstretched, ready to catch me as I jumped off. I landed right in his arms.

He lavished me with praise and congratulated me for my drum solo. I put my arms around him and we hugged until someone turned on the canned music. We danced and hung out together for the rest of the night until it was time for him to drive me home.

WILLIAM JAMES MACDONALD

The young man that I met was William James MacDonald. That was a pretty fancy name, I thought. Of course, to make things simpler he went by "Bill."

He was five years older than me, so I don't know why he was at our dance. He had long since graduated from high school. In fact, he hadn't even been a student at Bonnie Doon. He had gone elsewhere.

Bill was very nice, very respectful, and very pleasant. I enjoyed being with him and I knew I wanted to see him again. So when we arrived at my house in his 1963 Ford Galaxy, he asked me for my phone number. I gave it to him and we began dating.

He wasn't much of a drinker like I was, but we did attend lots of high school parties. There were a couple of times when I drank so much that he had to pretty much carry me out.

One time I had collapsed on someone's lawn, moaning and throwing up. But when I had made a mess of things he would just pick me up and gently place me in his car. Then we'd drive somewhere and sit so that I had a chance to sober up before I went home.

Who does that? He did. He was always kind and I needed that so much.

A SAD DAY

I worked for Phyllis for about a year and a half. One weekend, I was staying over there as usual and was surprised that she hadn't called me during the night to help her go to the bathroom. It was getting to be about nine or ten in the morning and I was still in bed and thought she should have been awake by now.

I got up and went out to the living room where her bed was and called her name. But there was no answer. I walked right up to her bed and spoke her name again, but still nothing. So I reached out and shook her a bit. No response.

Then I saw that she looked sort of strange. It occurred to me that she may have died but I couldn't admit that to myself.

After a moment or two, I called 911. I don't remember what I said, but the first responders were there within a few minutes. I got out of the way while they worked with her but it was no use; she had passed away during the night so they loaded her onto a stretcher and carried her out.

That was the first time I had ever seen or touched a dead person. The memory has never left me.

GRAB THE CASH

I had a telephone number for her family but I wasn't exactly sure how to handle the call or how *they* would handle it. But I made myself pick up the phone and dial.

Family members came to the apartment within the hour. They thanked me but I don't remember all that was said. I do remember waiting for her people to arrive.

As I sat there, it ran through my mind that Phyllis had some money stashed away on the top shelf of her closet. A voice was telling me that I could grab the cash and no one would ever know. I was horrified. My answer to the voice was, "No! I could never do that."

The truth is, that whole experience put me into a state of shock. I went numb inside and I couldn't feel any emotion for days. There was one thing I did feel though, and that was guilt. I felt guilty for being tempted to take Phyllis's money.

It took years for me to deal with that emotion but I did finally come to realize that temptation is not wrong. It's only when we *act* on temptation that it becomes wrong.

I did the right thing by not taking her money. I'm sure the guilt of stealing it would have plagued me for the rest of my life. Thankfully, I was not guilty of anything and I can live with that. I'm at ease about it and I thank God for helping me refuse to do that awful thing.

I was also grateful to have Bill by my side. We sat together many times while I shared my feelings and memories of Phyllis. At other times, I said nothing at all, but he was there. He was more of a friend to me than I ever realized.

CHAPTER ELEVEN

THE AUDITION

Let me backtrack to the Fall of 1974. After moving close to my new high school, I was looking forward to starting tenth grade. My school was having tryouts for the stage band, (also called a "big band"), and I wanted to be the drummer; I wanted it *badly.*

Tryout day came, I walked into the band room, and I saw nothing but lots of boys. Big boys, small boys, blonde boys, and dark-haired boys. They were there in every size and description you can imagine, and they were all there for the same reason. They also wanted to play drums in the big band. I said to myself, "Think again, boys. This gig is mine." (How's that for a shy, introverted girl?)

One after another they took the drummer's chair and with sticks in their hands, each one played for the director. Deep in my heart, I felt the job had to be mine because I was the hungriest.

Well, I was so impatient to take over that I finally stood up, went to the boy who was on the drum stool at the time, looked him straight in the eye, and firmly said, "Get off!" That was *way* out of character for me.

At my demand, (and I don't know how I was so bold), the boy looked at me like I was going to eat him alive. Without saying a word he got up and stood aside about three feet. Then I sat down and played.

It was just like that. And yes, I got the job ahead of all those boys in the room. I guess the director felt I was the best choice.

I *should* say I was shocked over getting "the chair" but I knew it was meant to be. Now, here I was, sitting before the director, playing the drums as if I had always been there. At long last, I was going to make music in a real, honest-to-goodness, band.

DREAM YOUR TROUBLES AWAY

I don't know if you can relate to this but it's sort of like dreaming in black and white. Everything is fuzzy and unreal. The dream makes sense and yet it doesn't.

Then, the black-and-white dream slowly begins to take on color, becoming more realistic. Finally, the dream explodes with hues, touching every part of you. That's when you know your dream is coming true. Do you see what I mean?

There's an old song written by Harry Barris Billy Moll and sung by people like Doris Day and Rosemary Clooney, that says:

> *"When skies are cloudy and gray*
> *They're only gray for a day*
> *So wrap your troubles in dreams*
> *And dream your troubles away"*

Well, my freshly painted dream had touched me and I knew that before it was over it was going to wrap me up in itself. There's nothing I can say to describe how that made me feel. In the simplest of terms, I would say, "I knew my dream had transformed into real life and this was just the beginning."

LIFE IN THE BAND

To be very honest, music class was the only reason I stayed in high school. Academics held zero interest for me. I often skipped my other classes and earned Cs and Ds in most of them.

The big band rehearsed two or three times a week and it was great. We had five trumpets, five trombones, an array of saxophones, and a rhythm section made up of piano, guitar, bass, and drums.

Our school had a "feeder" school, meaning that the junior high kids that eventually came our way were already schooled on their instruments, so by the time they arrived they could play. Our feeder school happened to be Strathern, where I spent grade seven!

BIG BANDS

Our director was a gifted trumpet player and had an amazing ear for music. He knew exactly what to do and how to get the best out of us, including me.

As music students, we spent our time studying big bands. At this point, I had been listening to mostly rock and pop music and I wasn't versed in the big band genre.

Woody Herman's band, known as "the band that plays the blues," was at the top of our list. We played a couple of his charts, like *La Fiesta* and *Alone Again, Naturally.* I'll tell you more about these songs in a minute.

And there was Maynard Ferguson, who was born in Montreal, Canada. He started playing piano and violin when he was only four years old. He went on to become a fantastic "screech" trumpet player. They called it that because he could play in extremely high registers. I saw him perform *live* in Toronto. He and his band were phenomenal.

There was also Benny Goodman who was known for his concert at Carnegie Hall in New York City on January 16, 1938, which was described by critic Bruce Eder as, "the single most important jazz or popular music concert in history."

Count Basie, jazz pianist, composer, and one of the greatest band leaders of his time was another talent we studied, learning how to play with his musical style. Later, in 1979, I saw him "live" at Place des Arts in Montreal. That was fantastic. These bands and others all played a big part in my music education and appreciation.

And I should mention a concert I saw when I was still just seventeen. I tried to get some friends to go with me but many of my friends didn't know who the lady singer was. So I went alone.

The concert was held at the Jubilee Auditorium (in Edmonton). My seat was on the main floor, about thirty rows back on the left side. In concert that evening was Ella Fitzgerald, Joe Pass, and Oscar Peterson. It was a monumental concert, forever burned into my mind.

I've seen a lot of shows, but I need to mention yet one more. Even though the legal drinking age in Edmonton was 18, our band director took our band class to a bar downtown to hear the funk band, Tower of Power.

I'm talking about ten black guys who played the most deep-down, funky rhythm and blues you've ever heard. It was loud, it was thumping, but it was oh, so skillful. Besides a rhythm section, they had saxes and horns.

Some of their hits included *You're Still A Young Man, What Is Hip, Bump City,* and *Down To The Night Club* to name a few.

Their horn section remained a much-in-demand backing group for some of pop/rock's biggest names, including Elton John, Santana, Bonnie Raitt, Huey Lewis, Little Feat, David Sanborn, Michelle Shocked, Paula Abdul, Aaron Neville, Aerosmith, and more. That band was the coolest thing I ever did hear.

TING–TING–A–TING

Back in high school, I was settling into my big band drumming job. To be honest, I didn't understand the "swing" patterns on the drum set, so the director took one of my sticks and played a rhythm on the cymbal. It was sort of a "ting-ting-a-ting, ting-a-ting" kind of sound.

He showed me what to do with my left hand at the same time, as well as with both of my feet. Then he gave me some records and said, "Take these home and listen to them and copy what they do."

Believe it or not, that was the only drum lesson I had when I was getting started. After that, I was able to play the different arrangements we were given. And I could read drum charts because I had learned to read music in junior high. So, I just continued to build my skills as an up-and-coming musician.

LEAVING ON A JET PLANE

As I mentioned, one of the songs we tackled was called *La Fiesta*. It was written by keyboard player, Chick Corea. But the song was made popular by several bands. We adopted the Woody Herman version on his album titled, *Giant Steps.*

At some point that year, Woody Herman and his big band came to our city and most of our band members went to see him. What a total thrill. (I still have the ticket stub.)

Well, the song mentioned is a quick jazz waltz written in three/four time. It was one of the songs we performed in competition.

We performed so well at the provincial level that our high school big band flew to Toronto that year to compete in the National Canadian Stage Band Festival. We came in second place in the nation. How terrific was that?

On that trip, I also met Phil Nimmons. He was born in Kamloops, British Columbia, and became a big band leader. He joined the University of Toronto in 1973, and in 2002 he received the Governor General's Performing Arts Award for his lifetime contribution to popular music. That award is Canada's highest honor given in the performing arts.

This honored and highly accomplished man, Phil Nimmons, pulled *me* aside backstage to ask me if I would be willing to stay in Toronto so he could work with me.

I thought, "Are you kidding me?" No, he wasn't kidding. This man, a giant in the musical field, wanted to train me, promote me as a musician, and teach me all that he knew about music and drums. My head was spinning.

It was the opportunity of a lifetime. But the truth is, at my core, I was afraid. I doubted that I would be good enough for him, and it scared me to think that in time he would discover my musical weaknesses and reject me.

I just couldn't have taken that kind of rejection so I told him, "my parents wouldn't go for it." Out of fear, I threw my chance away. I sometimes wonder what would have happened had I traveled that road.

That same year the festival organizers put together an all-star big band with all the top players from across the nation. I was chosen as one of the three top drummers. They put me on the drum set while the other two played percussion.

We had one rehearsal and then performed at the end of the event as a "feature band." I received an award plaque and was named one of the most outstanding drummers in Canada. I was only fifteen years old. How could I ever forget those days?

Little high school bands, big bands, national competitions, or just a few of us getting together to jam for a while; it didn't matter to me. I loved it all.

And the plaque? I still have it; it hangs on the wall in my office/music studio. Memories like that don't get left behind. I'll have them forever.

CHAPTER TWELVE

WORKING AT THE POST OFFICE

After Phyllis died, I decided to apply for a job at the post office. The entrance exam was grueling, but apparently, I did very well. During the interview, they said I scored in the top five percent and wanted to hire me. There was just one problem. I was only 15 and they couldn't take me until I turned 16.

Well, that was only a couple of months away. They told me to come back after my birthday and they'd hire me. And that's just what happened.

I worked from 4:30 to 9:00, five nights a week plus some weekends. I made a *lot* of money and liked the job. I worked in the parcel department, sorting packages that went all over the world.

The facility was huge. Besides the main floor where the public came in, there were two floors above ground and three more floors below ground. The lowest level is where all the magazines and junk mail was processed. They sent us there to work when we ran out of packages to sort and categorize.

I managed to do all of that and go to school, too. It was great because I could finally afford to buy all the stuff I wanted, like clothes and record albums. I even saved enough money to go to Hawaii the following year with Bill. I paid his way and mine and I gave him $1000 to spend.

I loved everything about Hawaii. The sun was magnificent and the heat was soothing for a couple of hours at a time. But then I'd have to get back into the air conditioning. It was a bit hot for this Alberta, girl.

My post office job made all of that possible and I still dream about the place. I envision all the conveyer belts and the huge steel glacier where the canvas bags full of mail come sliding down from the loading docks. I held that job for two years until I was done with school.

PRISON COULD HAVE BEEN MY FUTURE

As a teenager, I was like all the other kids. Almost everyone drank alcohol, took drugs, and had either boyfriends or girlfriends. Many of us could go to the bar with no questions asked. The legal drinking age was 18 but we looked so grown up at 16 and 17 years old that we had no problem getting served.

My boyfriend and I found that we could get served anywhere. Years later when I was 23, I was finally asked for I.D. I said,

"Are you kidding me? You're asking me *now*, after all these years?!"

The waitress just shrugged and I laughed out loud as I handed her my driver's license.

Sometimes I would meet my friends after work at the lounge in the MacDonald Hotel downtown. We'd drink and have a good time.

After a while, I sold marijuana there. To me, it was just a natural progression from the way the rest of my life was going. A guy at school sold me a pound of weed which I divided up into smaller bags and sold downtown, by the ounce.

I had the drugs stored in an empty locker at the post office. Of course, I had to carry it right past the security guard at the front door, but somehow that didn't concern me.

Here I was selling drugs out of a locker on federal property and walking right past a federal guard to get it in and get it out again. I could have gone to prison for that--for years--but I guess God wasn't allowing prison life to be part of my future.

I did eventually become involved in prison life but as a minister. Today, many years later, my husband and I have a successful prison ministry. I always try to reassure the inmates that I am no better than they are. I tell them, "You and I are not different at all except for one thing . . . I never got caught."

STILL WINNING

The tenth grade was great. We had a winning stage band and a wonderful director. Unfortunately, Mr. Jenner didn't stay. He was a gifted salesman and left school to go back into that field, selling musical instruments.

Thankfully, another great leader came along. Mr. Smith. He took over and continued what Mr. Jenner had begun.

The next two years were successful for us. We didn't make it to the nationals for my 11th-grade year, but we did go back to Toronto to compete during my 12th grade year.

Again, that third time, we placed in the top three in the country. We had some fantastic players and I'll always remember how great it was to play with them.

So what happened in 11th grade? Well, the fact that we didn't get past the provincial competition was probably my fault. Really? Yes, I blamed myself, and I'm afraid my band was upset with me, too, although they were very kind at the time.

HEY JUDE

We were set up in a huge arena for the competition and there must have been over 4,000 people there; that's my guess. It was a major event for us high school kids. We were having the time of our lives.

Anyway, we were playing a song called *Hey Jude*, by the Beatles. At the end of the song, there was a long "ad-lib" section. The music ramped up and the soloists built the music into a crazy frenzy. I felt like I was playing on another planet, way out in the stratosphere. It was pure ecstasy.

But all good things have to come to an end, even this. So when we got to the very end of the song, the director gave the signal to abruptly cut us off. But guess what? I missed the signal.

On one single note--in unison--the whole band stopped playing. That is, everyone except me. I was lost in my own little world, just me and my drums playing in one of the biggest venues ever. But at that moment, all 4,000 pairs of eyes were on me.

Then I woke up and realized I was the only one playing. My playing then sort of petered out and I came to a stop. I was so embarrassed. The damage was done. Needless to say, we didn't score very high that day.

When we got backstage, I was crying, but the guys in the band gathered around me with hugs and encouraging words. They were great. I appreciated their comfort and understanding but I knew I had made the worst mistake of my life.

What a great bunch of people they were. I may not remember names or even all the faces, but I'll never forget their support. Thankfully, I don't think I've ever gaffed like that again. I've always been able to cover up my errors. Somehow, after that horrible incident, I did manage to recover my confidence and go on playing to achieve more victories.

As a band, we did very well in my final year of school. One of the songs we tackled was a song written in 13/4 time, a very complicated time signature. I believe the title was, *The Great Divide*, by Don Ellis; it was quite challenging.

We once performed it inside a three-level shopping mall. All the musicians, except for the rhythm section, split up to play from various balconies on the different floors. It was a very unique and exciting piece of music. And it sharpened us into winning competitors once again.

MY WORLD OF BOYFRIENDS

While music filled my world, I still had time for dating but I was getting restless with my boyfriend, Bill. He was very good to me, but the "spark" was gone. (I had so much to learn back then.) Even though we had talked about getting married one day, I knew in my heart, he wasn't the one.

I came to the place where I decided to break things off. I told him what a great guy he was, but . . . I wanted to move on. I know it really hurt him but I couldn't continue with him anymore.

Several years later I heard he got married. They had a huge wedding to the tune of $40,000. There were 1000 guests, they hired musicians from the Edmonton Symphony, and rented a Rolls Royce for their "get-away car." I also heard their marriage only lasted a couple of years. I felt bad for him.

In the meantime, I started dating Cliff. He played trombone in the school stage band. His parents liked me. Even after Cliff and I had broken up, his dad agreed to co-sign my car loan because my mother wouldn't do it.

Cliff and I dated for less than one year. Then I met Pete. I had been out of school a few months by then and was working at a gas station as a cashier. He was a mechanic there. I'll tell you about him in chapter 13.

NEW HORIZONS

When high school ended in 1977, I thought my big band days were over. But then I heard that the City of Edmonton had a big band, so I went to audition for them.

When I got there, I guess my reputation as a drummer preceded me because the director of the band already knew of me and accepted me right then and there. I was floored.

Here I was barely 18 years old and I was going to be part of the city's big band; a city with a metro area of half a million people. (Today in 2023, the population has tripled to one and a half million.)

Then, when the director informed me of the practice schedule, it hit me. This was real! My dreams were coming true.

The band leader, Mr. Harry Pinchin, was a fine, professional trumpet player with the Tommy Banks orchestra. Banks was also a big band leader and a phenomenal piano player and was in demand all over Western Canada. But not *only* in Canada. They played extensively, all over the world.

Tommy Banks hosted national and international, syndicated, and network television programs, including *The Tommy Banks Show, Somewhere There's Music, What's My Name, Love and Mr. Smith, Celebrity Revue, Symphony of a Thousand, Tommy Banks Jazz,* and more. What a busy guy.

He provided musical direction for the ceremonies of the XI Commonwealth Games, EXPO '86, The World University Games, the XV Olympic Winter Games, and for countless television shows. He has even played for Presidents of the United States, and the Queen of England.

Harry Pinchin, as a band director, had already been receiving awards for 10 years or more, but during that year alone, 1978, he was Band Director for the official band of Athlete's Village for the Commonwealth Games. He received the Alberta Achievement Award of Excellence as CMS Director, and the National Music Award, for the Canadian Band Association, as director.

For the next 20 years or more Pinchin was still receiving awards as Director of Canadian Big Bands. So no, I can hardly tell you what an honor it was for me to be associated with this band, knowing whom I was connected with.

CHAPTER THIRTEEN

ONE "TEENY" PROBLEM

There *is* a little twist to my story . . . After I was invited to fill the drummer's chair for the City of Edmonton, I had one "teeny" little problem: I didn't have a drum set. How was I going to fix this?

The first thing I did was go down to Lillo's Music on 82nd Avenue. I picked out a set of Ludwig drums with Zildjian cymbals, high-hats, heavy-duty Tama stands, and of course, sticks. It was a complete set. They had a butcher block finish, just like the drums we had at school. I paid about $700 for the whole shebang. I still have the receipt.

Then I realized I had another problem. Even after I bought the drums, I had no way to transport them. That's when I decided it was time to buy a car. I was still working at the post office, so I was able to get credit. Also, after much thought and discussion with guys at work, I decided to buy a Volkswagen, Rabbit. So I went straight to the local Volkswagen dealer and saw the perfect car.

It was the Fall of 1977 and the new models were just coming out. As I stood there in the showroom, looking like I had done this all my life, I talked to a salesman, pointed to the white model on display, and said, "I want *that* one!" Yup. I bought a white, 1978 Rabbit, brand new, right off of the showroom floor. Nothing to it, right?

When the paperwork was done, a man moved the car outside for me, and the keys were handed over, and there I was, a proud automobile owner. Wow. I had a brand new set of Ludwig drums and a brand-new car. Could life get any better?

JUST ONE MORE THING

Okay, well that's all fine, but I had one more fly in the ointment: I didn't have a driver's license; I didn't even know how to drive . . . but yes, I was going to learn, by golly, and I was going to learn fast.

The dealership delivered the car to my house and it sat in the back driveway while I spent the next two weeks taking driving lessons.

I enjoyed the lessons, first because I liked driving, but second, my instructor had been a professional drummer for Moe Koffman for 18 years. How cool was *that?*

Moe Koffman was a jazz saxophonist and flutist, composer, and arranger, who played with Jimmy Dorsey and other big bands. He was considered one of Canada's most prolific musicians with a career spanning from 1950 into the 2000s. He was famous for the song titled, *Swingin' Shepheard Blues.*

So, my driving instructor played drums for Moe Koffman for almost two decades. And we talked more about drums than we did about the rules of the road. But it was all good. I passed everything and became legal to drive.

Believe it or not, I managed to get my entire drum set into the back of that little car. So I was off to band rehearsals with my new drums in my new car. Life was taking shape as I had always wanted it to. What else could an 18-year-old kid want?

How did I get here? How did this all happen? I realized many years later that God was ordering my steps because this trail of events doesn't just happen every day to a young, inexperienced girl. Now all that remained to be seen was, "How would I handle my blessings?"

THE MAILBAG AND ME

For the rest of the year, until about December of 1977, I continued my job in the parcel section of the post office during the day and played in the band at night. Then I transferred from working inside the plant to becoming a letter carrier.

After a couple of weeks of training, I was sent out, on foot, into the freezing cold, with a 50-pound mail bag hanging on my shoulder. What was I *thinking?*

The day I began working outside, the temperature was about minus 30. In Edmonton, these extremely cold temps are common. We would see bouts of frigid air like this each month or so. The in-between, temps would vary between freezing and about minus ten degrees. It was miserable. (By the way, we're talking Fahrenheit.)

To make a long story short, I lasted roughly six weeks fighting the cold with the heavy mail bag digging into my shoulder.

Then one day during lunch hour I decided I had enough. I walked into my station with my uniform in hand and said, "Bye!"

I explained that I absolutely could not take it anymore. They scolded me for leaving them without notice but I couldn't help it. The weather was miserable, the job was miserable, and I was miserable. It was time to put an end to it.

WORKING AT THE CAR WASH

I had to find a new job right away but I was very unskilled and didn't possess a high school diploma. Yes, I went thru all 12 years but my grades were pitifully low and I was short the credits I needed to graduate.

So, there I was with loans on both my car and my drums and I was determined I was not going to lose either one of them. I had to find work.

Finding a job in the middle of winter in Canada was not an easy task. The only job I could find was at a local car wash, making $7.00 an hour. Compared to my previous post office salary, that was really small potatoes, but I had to do it.

I ended up working at Splash 'N Dash for a whole year. It was really hard work, and I was skinnier than a rail at the end of it all, (weighing in at about 115 pounds). But I made it and always kept up with my payments. Thank goodness I was still living at home and didn't have to pay rent.

MY FRIEND DARRYL

Let me tell you about my friend, Darryl. I met him in the summer of 1977, at a party given at his house which Pete (my new boyfriend) and I had attended. While Pete was showing off his knife-twirling skills and talking shop with the boys, I was sitting next to Darryl as we spun records and talked about music all night long.

He had tons of records; a couple of thousand I think. And he had broad musical tastes. Of course, we listened to the rock music of the day, as well as imported rock (from Europe), progressive rock, blues, jazz, soul, and R&B. He was a bass player and I had played with him a few times at jam sessions.

Darryl and I became lifelong friends until his passing about 14 years later.

While Darryl and I were friends, I was dating Pete. We met at the first gas station I worked at. He was tall, muscular, dark, and kind of handsome. Our dates usually consisted of going to parties. There was always lots of drinking going on. And there were drugs, too, like pot, hash, cocaine, and sometimes LSD, (acid).

It was said that Pete could drop ten hits of acid at one time. I guess that's possible; I don't know. He was a big guy, so biologically speaking, I guess he could take it. I never saw him do it, but I was with him plenty of times when he was under the influence.

I found LSD to be an interesting drug. It creates all kinds of imaginings that seem very real. Some people have "bad trips;" that is always a risk.

Pot was another story. I didn't like it because it made me paranoid. Whereas alcohol gave me the extra confidence I needed to be the life of the party, pot and hash did the opposite. It made me self-conscious and that led to defeatism and feelings of worthlessness.

I tried several kinds of drugs (except those used with needles) but they made me hyper so I didn't do much of them. I found that just sticking to good old whiskey was the ticket for me.

A SAD VIOLATION

Another detail I would just as soon forget has to do with Pete. He would come into the gas station on Saturdays to work on his own car. When I didn't have customers, I'd go out to the bays to watch him.

We talked a bit and we sort of liked each other. I was attracted to him because he was like a "daddy" figure to me. I saw things in him I loved about my real dad and before too long we became a couple.

Halfway into our courtship, Pete decided to assault me. One night while I was working evenings at the gas bar, he came in with his buddy, shuffled me away from the cash register, and pushed me into the back office. He told his buddy to "mind the store" as he shut the door behind us.

It didn't take but a minute for me to realize what was on his mind. As he pulled and pawed at me I realized he intended to force himself on me. Even though I fought him he was too strong.

He acted like an ugly, unfeeling, cruel beast. I tried to make him stop but he proceeded against my will. Thank the Lord I was not physically hurt.

I include this story only to help those who fall into this trap; especially young women. When someone grows up experiencing abuse, that abuse becomes normalized; that is, the person will stay in an abusive relationship because it seems "normal."

Furthermore, their desire to avoid loneliness is greater than their need to be respected. How tragic.

For that reason, I could not explain at the time, why I continued seeing this man. But the day came when he said he was tired of me . . . And so, after almost a year . . . that was it. He walked out of my life for good. I was crushed.

The truth is, I should have seen it as a blessing because it was for *my* good. But instead, I shut myself in my bedroom for a couple of days and sobbed. I don't know what his hold was on me, but my pain was very deep. I was so lost and there was a high price tag attached to my stupid mistakes.

My mother was worried but I never shared my troubles with her. I knew I hadn't been living right and I didn't want to expose all of that to her.

CHAPTER FOURTEEN

REACHING OUT

Now that I was done with school and past the age of 18, I started thinking about my real dad again. While my mother had won full and exclusive custody of me in a court settlement ten years earlier, I was no longer her responsibility. I was now a grown adult and had not seen my real father in all these years.

My mother believed she was doing the right thing and was protecting me at the time. But now that I had come of age, I was free to contact my real dad if I wanted to. But the question was; did I want to?

The answer was, yes. I had yearnings in my heart like any child would, being away from a parent for over a decade. There was a new mission before me. The thing to do now was to make a break from western Canada and take that long trip to Montreal.

I didn't even know if my dad was alive or not. And if he was alive, was he was still living in the same place? How would I find him?

There was a lot to search out and it would take some work, but a child should never be deprived of that connection. It's a necessity for peace of heart and mind and I was no different from any other person. So, hard-headed as I am, I made up my mind to look for him.

I went to the public library where they had stacks of phone books from other cities. (There was no internet back then.) I found the Montreal phone book and looked up my dad's name. It was there! Yes. Unbelievable. And he had the same address and phone number that we had when I lived there as a child.

I didn't want to call him because I thought that would be too shocking so I wrote him a letter. I didn't

know if I would hear anything back but in a short time--to my delight--I received a letter in the mail.
Here's what it said:

Dear Daughter,

I am very happy to hear from you after so many years, but to be a good Debreceni, I was waiting for your letter because I know my own blood and you are part of it. I would be more happier if you would live in the neighborhood . . .

I am still not a very good letter writer and I think it would be best if you could give us a telephone call and reverse the charges . . .

I would like very much to hear from you as soon as possible, my little mosquito . . .

Your loving father

A LITTLE VISIT

Wow. After all this time, my dad was interested in me. I was so happy. Of course, I had to tell my mom and my stepdad but I broke it to them gently and they understood.

There were other details in the letter. He told me he was remarried and they had a little girl. Her name was Sylvia and she was six years old. That's just about the same age I was when my parents split.

After all this time I wondered what my dad looked like and I was curious about my sister, too. Would she look like me?

We talked on the phone and then my Dad invited me to come for a visit and he would pay my way. So he flew me to Montreal where we met at the Dorval (now Trudeau) Airport. He and my godmother, Ava, came to meet me and when I saw him, I had a flood of emotions that are hard to describe.

We traveled from the airport to my dad's house in Brossard. It was the same house but with a few upgrades. There, I greeted his new wife, Margo, and my new sister. My godfather, Louie, was also there as we all sat down in the living room to look at each other and talk.

The Bible mentions the stress Jesus had in the Garden of Gethsemane that caused him to sweat drops of blood. Well, I didn't *sweat* blood, but the stress of it caused me to start hemorrhaging blood from my nose.

My godmother helped me to the bathroom and explained that it was the intensity of the moment causing my nosebleed; there was nothing physically wrong with me. She said the trip by air coupled with the anxiety created a strong reaction to the situation. With her help, it was soon over and I was fine. But I still had to face a Dad I hardly knew and a sister I had never met.

It was a good visit overall. I think I stayed about a week. Then I went back to Edmonton and wondered what I should do with the rest of my life.

ON MY OWN

When I got back home I decided it was time to move out on my own. I found an inexpensive studio apartment in a rather nice building. I was close to my friend, Darryl, and I could easily walk from my place to his. Our friendship was a special one.

I had a couple of different types of jobs during that time. First I tried telemarketing, of all things. It lasted two weeks. I hated it. I can do a lot of things but selling stuff is not one of my gifts. I am not "outgoing" by nature and can be a bit awkward. So that was out.

Then I got a job as a clerk in a "sheet-music store." I didn't have to persuade people to buy anything. They would come in already knowing what they wanted. I just had to be familiar with the products.

I left the music store after almost a year to work for an advertising company. My job was to organize a route-map, and dispatch sales personnel. I loved doing that because I got to organize the operation.

"Organization" should be my middle name. I am compelled to put things in order, even to this day. Maybe that talent had grown out of my need to fix my chaotic life.

THE STICK SHIFT!

While working for the advertising company, I was asked to run errands now and then, and chauffeur the "big boss" around when he came up from Vancouver. I figured he liked my efficiency and my personality because he asked me if I'd be willing to deliver a vehicle to his home and then drive him to Seattle, Washington, for business.

The deal was, I would drive his VW bus from Edmonton to Vancouver, pick him up, and take him across the border into the states. So just to be clear, the road between the two cities is about 780 miles, and takes roughly 13 hours of straight driving to get there. Furthermore, two-thirds of the journey wind through the Rocky Mountains.

To add misery to the situation, the VW bus was a standard shift vehicle. I had only ever driven an automatic. But what could go wrong, right?

I wasn't smart enough to travel early in the day, and so I found myself in the Rockies in the middle of the night.

Around two in the morning, I became very sleepy. All of a sudden I saw barricades blocking the road up ahead. I slammed on the brakes only to see the image vaporize and disappear.

When the whole scenario happened again, I realized I was hallucinating so I pulled over to the side of the road and slept for two hours.

As for the stick shift, it wasn't too hard to operate on the highway, but the cities were a killer, especially when I got to Vancouver. That city consists of endless rolling hills and often, I nearly smashed into the cars behind me because I couldn't prevent rolling backward while trying to accelerate forward. Finally, I put a "caution" sign on the back of the bus saying, *"Student Driver with Standard Shift,"* or something like that.

HE LOOKED LIKE A "MAFIA" MAN

I picked up the big boss and together we loaded ourselves into his car, (an automatic--thank goodness), and headed for the U.S. border.

We made pleasant chit-chat for the next hour until we reached the last road to the crossing gate. We waited in a line of cars for a bit and then it was our turn to roll up to the guard shack.

The border-guard spoke to me first, asking me all the usual questions like my name, where I was from, and why I wanted to enter the United States. I answered and explained I was driving Mr. _____, to Seattle for business.

Now, I won't exactly say the big boss was a "Mafia guy," but looking at him, the officer knew something didn't *smell* right. So, after my boss gave his name, the officer said,

"Sir, please step out of the vehicle. You will need to come inside for further questioning."

I learned later on through the Edmonton office that the man had served 18 years in prison for armed robbery and they still had his name on their rosters. They denied him entry into the U.S. and we had to turn back to Vancouver. At least the company was nice enough to pay for my airfare home.

Oh, the wisdom of an 18-year-old. I was so naive.

HEADING EAST

Sometime around my nineteenth birthday, I quit the advertising company and decided to move to Montreal to be with my real Dad, long term. I didn't pack a lot of stuff so I must have stored many of my belongings at my parents' house.

As I put my clothes and my record collection in my car I was excited to be on my way. This was the same trip my mom and Alex and I made by car years before, but now I was going in the opposite direction; going home you might say.

The trip was over 2,200 miles. The eastbound drive from Edmonton across the prairies was quite boring. The land is flat all the way to western Ontario. There's nothing to see except miles and miles of stretched-out wheat, corn, and canola fields. There are a few little towns along the way and a couple of large cities like Regina and Winnipeg.

Finally, Thunder Bay began to peak out of the flat lands displaying beautiful landscapes and rolling hills. Montreal was in my crosshairs but I still had a ways to go.

OUT OF THE DARKNESS

I had been driving for almost three days. That third night I was very tired so I pulled off into a little area carved out of the side of the highway. It was far enough into the bushes that I thought it would lend me the privacy I needed to get some rest. It was midnight.

I folded down the back seat so I'd have a bit more room to stretch out. Then I curled up, and off to sleep I went.

Because I normally sleep like a rock it was unusual for me to have stirred, but at about two o'clock in the morning, I woke up for no particular reason. In a moment, I was wide awake. I was not groggy and my nerves from my head to my toes were tingling.

I peered out the windows in every direction, straining my eyes to see as much as I could. There was still nothing but darkness all around.

Then I sat fully upright hoping to have a better look. All I saw was a bunch of trees silhouetted against the dark sky.

Then, about a hundred feet away in that thick foreboding black air, I spotted something moving. I was thinking it might be a large animal, but a distinct form appeared and it moved closer. Then I realized it was a person slowly moving toward my car.

Quietly and just as covertly as the night was covering him, this sinister, hunched-over figure walked left to right and right to left in a semi-circular pattern, bringing himself closer and closer to my vehicle.

I could feel, see, and sense his evil intentions as he got closer, stalking me like a hunter stalking his prey.

If ever I've been sure of a sixth sense it was at that moment. I had no doubt he intended to harm me.

Fear rose to a fevered pitch. Like a screaming in my chest, and in my mind, I knew that I had to make a move now, or be seriously harmed . . . or worse.

MY KEYS!

My car had a flat hatch-back door which allowed access into the car from the rear. The man continued his trek until finally, he was staring at me through my back window; his face was no more than two feet from mine.

Then his hand moved slowly toward the handle and the trouble is, I couldn't remember whether or not I had locked it.

Adrenaline suddenly kicked in and I jumped into the front seat hoping to start the car and drive away. I was *so thankful* to find that I had left the keys in the ignition. Without wasting a second I was able to start the engine and take off out of there as fast as I could.

My foot was "pedal to the metal" as they say. I careened my way out of the bushes and onto the highway as my wheels kicked up dirt and debris behind me.

My heart was still pounding with fear and my mind was screaming, "Get away, get away!" At the same time, I was wailing, "Oh God in heaven. Oh, God! Oh, God!!"

Just as suddenly as it had happened, it was over. The last I saw of him was that fearful image in my rear-view mirror, as he stood there in the darkness staring after me. Then he was out of my sight.

My nerves let loose and I broke into a flood of tears as I sped down the road heading eastward. I cried out to the Lord over the next few hours as I drove on into the night. I was chilled down into my spirit, imagining what could have happened if I hadn't woken up.

I was convinced that it was God who woke me up and saved my life because nothing else made sense. I was a heavy sleeper, I was comfortable, and I was tired. There's no good, logical reason I awakened in time to get out of there.

While I had abandoned God, I know God hadn't abandoned me. He was still taking care of me. Why?

THE GAS STATION MAN

The sun was just beginning to rise as I pulled into some little town. I was exhausted, both from driving and from crying. I saw a gas station up ahead and pulled in, hoping they were open.

The owner was just getting his night lights turned off for the day, and he spotted me through the glass door. He came out to talk to me, and as he did he could see how upset I was.

At the same time, I had gotten out of the car so I could check my hatchback door. I was curious to know if I had locked it. I pushed the button and the door opened. It was *not locked.* Oh, my God.

I was shaken to the bone and I kept wiping my face trying to stop the tears as I blurted out what I had encountered in the bushes during the night. He finally offered to let me pull my car inside, into one of his work bays.

He told me he wasn't going to be open for another hour but he suggested I should at least try to get a little bit of sleep in the safety of his garage.

Somehow, I trusted him and agreed. I pulled my car into the bay and he locked the door behind me. Here I was: my car was locked in a gas station garage with a strange man I knew nothing about yet I felt safe and at peace.

I was comfortable enough and was able to rest for that short hour before I had to be on my way. Many times through the years I've thought about that man and I am so grateful for his kindness.

CHAPTER FIFTEEN

DAD'S HOUSE

With the road before me, I continued on my way again, crossing through the rest of Ontario into Quebec. Then I turned south toward Montreal. What a night; what an ordeal. All I could say was, "Thank you God for helping me get this far."

I reached my Dad's house late that evening not knowing what to expect. I pulled up to the house my Mom and I lived in, where I was raised for a few of my earliest years of life.

Mom, Dad, and me. That's the way it was back then. But everything had drastically changed. I knew it wasn't my home anymore so, I kind of felt like a stranger or an intruder.

The house now belonged to my father, his new wife, Margo, and their young daughter, Sylvia. Margo had two older children from another marriage but her son had moved out on his own, and her daughter had just married.

I went to the front door and knocked. They were expecting me but I still hoped they would receive me after my long trip.

Thankfully, Dad and his wife, Margo, greeted me warmly. He asked me how the trip was and I told him about my harrowing experience when I was parked off the highway in the trees. To my surprise, he laughed. I'm not sure why, but I know it wasn't that he didn't care. He just thought I was stupid, pulling off, alone in the bush like that. I guess I was.

Yes, it probably served me right. I learned my lesson though. I was never going to do *that* again. Now, I had other things to learn. Now, I had to decide what I was going to do with myself. What kind of a life was I going to have?

I didn't have much money and needed a job and a place to live. Where should I begin? I knew it would be a challenge but I made this move; now I had to make the best of it.

SWEEPING THE FLOORS

After a few days of welcomed rest, Dad took me several miles across town to his shop and handed me a broom. He was inviting me to go to work for him and wanted me to start from the bottom and work my way up.

My dad always wanted a son to take over his business someday. But all he had were two daughters: me and Sylvia. He hoped I would become interested in his business and let my curiosity lead me into all aspects of the trade so that I might take a principal role in his operations in the future.

He was a highly skilled tool and die maker, creating injection molds for manufacturing plastics and he was well-known in the industry. He had contracts in Canada and the United States and his company was no small potatoes.

For now, my job was to sweep the floors, so sweep the floors I did. It was income and it would provide me with the independence I needed. So far so good.

In the evenings, after work, I would go back to my dad's house for supper and sleep. He gave me one of the bedrooms and to the best of my memory, the house hadn't changed a whole lot since I lived there as a child, eleven years ago.

One nice addition was the in-ground pool they added in the backyard. It was a pretty, kidney-shaped pool with a diving board and a slide. I took advantage of it on hot summer days, although I never could figure out why they never heated the water. Oh well.

In later years they did make a few more upgrades. A wall was removed between two of the upstairs bedrooms, making it into one big room for my sister. They also remodeled the kitchen and upstairs bathroom, complete with recessed lighting.

ON MY OWN AGAIN

I was glad to be around my dad after missing him all those years but at the same time, he was a tough customer to get along with. He didn't like the way I did things, the hours I kept, and other such things that I, as a young woman, felt I had a right to do. I just couldn't please him no matter what I did or how hard I tried.

To be fair, I was quite rowdy and I liked to stay out late with friends from work. Living like that as the daughter of the company's owner probably did create a poor image in front of his employees. I know I got on his nerves and his new wife Margo felt the same way.

So, I began to hunt for an apartment, a place of my own, a place where I could do as I pleased without being controlled.

Lo and behold, I found an apartment in the northern part of Montreal, on Bloomfield Street. That's the very same street I lived on when I was two years old.

My apartment was across the street and down a few buildings from where we lived back then. How amazing is that? Way back in the beginning of their marriage Mom and Dad and I had lived on this street and now I was back here on my own.

MY PLACE

My little apartment was what you might call an "efficiency." I had a living room/bedroom combination, a bathroom, and a small kitchen. It was on the second floor facing the street, and it was near the corner.

It would get pretty noisy at night due to thin walls and lots of street noise. But to be honest, sometimes I would get loud myself, spinning my records or playing my guitar until some other tenant would bang on the wall for me to shut the "blankety-blank" up.

Oh, and there were bugs. Lots of them. They drove me crazy. My only hope for any comfort was when the exterminator came, about every three months, spraying insecticide into every nook and cranny. That would reduce the pest population for at least a little while.

So, this was my new place and my new life. Work, eat, sleep, and wonder what else there was to do.

QUE SERA SERA

I liked to drive around by myself and explore Montreal. I learned where a lot of the streets were, and there were certain shops I liked to visit.

Sometimes, I would drive all the way downtown, to a particular cigar shop, just to buy a copy of Rolling Stone Magazine. Other times I'd drive to the various neighborhoods I lived in as a child and strange waves of nostalgia would sweep over me as I remembered all the old familiar places.

I recalled the Cote Des Neige area. I drove by the tall building my mom and I lived in (on the eighth floor). I remembered how we used to have salmon steak lunches at the cafeteria of the Jewish General Hospital on "fish Friday."

I thought about how Nagymama and I used to walk to Saint Joseph's Cathedral on hot summer days. And one time, we stopped at a portrait studio on the way, to have our pictures taken. My dad still displays those photos in his home.

The memories swept over me as I dreamed of my life back then. But, as the French say, "Que sera, sera," meaning, "Whatever will be will be." Once the years have passed us by, all we can do is accept things and go on. The past is unchangeable, but the future can become whatever we make of it.

MAKING NEW MEMORIES

Besides driving around, I liked to park downtown on St. Catherine Street and walk from Avenue Papineau to the Forum on St. Catherine's and Atwater street. That was about four miles each way and took me a good part of the day.

St. Catherine's is a very unique street. It changes from the elite and expensive restaurants and shopping boutiques on the west side to what is known as "skid-row" on the east side, where the homeless drunks, thieves, and drug addicts hang out, looking for spare change.

When I still lived at my dad's house I would head out in the morning from Brossard and cross the Jacques Cartier Bridge. (Jacques is pronounced with a kind of blunt "Sh-aahk" sound; *Cartier* is pronounced, *Car-tee-aye.)*

About this bridge: construction began on it in 1925 and cost 23 million dollars to complete. It was finished in two and a half years and is five lanes wide and over three miles long. Approximately 36 million vehicles cross it every year. What a sight to see.

Once over the bridge, I'd drive north a few blocks and park somewhere on St. Catherine's. Then I'd walk. I loved to stop at a certain bookstore about halfway down for coffee and a pastry. Then on the way back, as I neared the bridge again, I'd stop in all the "dime stores" to buy cheap, plastic accessories to decorate my new apartment.

One late afternoon, I was out shopping as usual. When I got to the Forum, I noticed that the band, Chicago, was about to start playing. I love Chicago! So I went to the box office, bought a ticket, and with my bags and parcels in tow, went in, sat down, and took in the concert.

They played many of their hit songs, like, *Saturday In the Park,* and *Does Anybody Really Know What Time it is?* What an absolute treat that was.

By the way, the Forum was built in 1924 by the Canadian Arena Company. It took only 159 days to complete. For the next 72 years it was used by Canadian hockey teams and all the games were televised from there. Of course, they would adjust the venue for live concerts. Later, it became a multiplex cinema.

FAMILY DRAMA

After I moved out on my own, I would still visit my dad and my sister on the weekends. They always had good food, and I enjoyed the beautiful pool in the backyard.

Sometimes they'd visit friends, either at their house, or at Dad's, and I'd join them. Unfortunately, there was usually a lot of drinking going on. My dad and his wife, Margo, would get soused, and then the arguing and the fighting would start. That's usually when the visiting would come to an end.

This is something my sister had to live with all of her life. I personally did not have the backbone to survive that kind of environment but somehow she did. And in that respect, I always thought she was much stronger than me.

But before Sylvia came along, there were Margo's two children from her first marriage, George and Margaret. They were placed in an orphanage for about four years because Margo couldn't care for them after she and her first husband separated.

When Margo married my father, George and Margaret moved in with them. But they had to endure a lot of craziness in the home such as drinking and fighting.

When Sylvia was born, Margaret often found herself having to look after the child because Margo was incapacitated.

George became fed up with it all and moved out, and Margaret wanted to go back to the orphanage. She said she was treated well there. But it didn't happen.

When she turned 18, she married Leslie, our long-time family friend, and Sylvia was left alone. She said she felt abandoned and that made her very sad. Unfortunately, the family drama continued.

CHAPTER SIXTEEN

BUCKETS, BUTTONS, SWEATERS, AND KNOBS

I lived in the Montreal area for almost three years. During that time--little by little--I was getting my VW Rabbit paid off. I held down three jobs, not out of necessity but because I had nothing better to do.

All my jobs were in manufacturing. I still worked for my dad during the day, but I took an evening job in a bucket factory. Yup, a bucket factory. And then on the weekends, I worked in a button factory. Right again.

The button factory also handled electro-plating; they received plastic parts like knobs for appliances and sort of baked them in a kind of solution making them look shiny or chromed.

At some point I worked a *temp* job in a sweater factory, folding sweaters to be packaged and shipped to various stores across the country.

Buckets, buttons, sweaters, and knobs. What an exciting life, right? I wasn't lazy, for sure. I was rather a "go-getter" and have been all my life. Anyway, the combined income was good and it gave me something to do.

Montreal is known for its many factories so work was easy to find. The downside to these jobs was the type of people I met that I called "friends." I'm not saying that hourly laborers are bad people but I am saying that among them are a fair number of "riff-raff" types and somehow I would always find them. Or rather, they found me.

THE WHISTLEBLOWER

I remember that I started dating a man from Haiti who spoke mostly French. I guess I went with him for six or eight months. I didn't think I was doing anything wrong; he worked for my dad but I didn't realize how badly it reflected on him to have his daughter going out with the hired help.

I personally don't have anything against mixed-race couples. So for me, the race factor was not an issue but it was for my dad.

More importantly, the boy didn't have the best character, and that *was* an issue, but I couldn't see it. I didn't think there was anything wrong with our relationship but then I didn't have a whole lot of respect for myself. Deep down, I felt kind of worthless. How sad.

Why? Because so many times, growing up, I was told I was stupid and couldn't do anything right. That destroyed my confidence. It made me feel unworthy and it scarred me, emotionally. My sensitive personality couldn't survive the criticism and rejection.

Anyway, I made the mistake of sharing my escapades with Margo. I told her I was dating this guy from the shop and it wasn't too long before she told my father.

Why I ever told her, I don't know. I guess I just needed someone to confide in. A *friend* if you will. I didn't expect her to tell my dad but I guess she was just trying to look out for me. Things did *not* go well with Dad after that and he let me know it. He definitely was *not* happy about it.

I hated being in trouble with my father, but even so, I always did what I wanted to do no matter who didn't like it. I had to do things my way regardless of what the result would be. I was still stuck with that "what if" syndrome and the only way to see what would happen was to try it, even if it meant rebellion.

IN TROUBLE AGAIN

After that relationship ended, I dated another one of my dad's employees for a brief time. I guess that's because these were the only people I knew socially, so they were the ones I befriended.

This time it was one of my dad's shop foremen. Somehow, word got back to Margo again and this time she sent a spy to my apartment to see if it was true. It was. He came to the door and saw the man inside.

She blew the whistle on me one more time. That was the last straw for Dad! When he found out he was spitting mad.

I stopped by the house one day for some reason and he met me at the door. I came in as far as the top of the staircase but no further. With his arms flailing in the air and his face red with anger, he confronted me, screaming all kinds of obscenities. It was hard and it was harsh and it crushed me. That's when he told me to get out and that he never wanted me to step foot in his house again.

Not too long ago, Sylvia and I talked about that incident. She remembered it well. She said it was awful and it made her very sad. She didn't see me again for a long time after that and she felt abandoned and alone just like she had when her half-brother and half-sister moved out.

Yes, I deserved what I got, but it was still difficult to bear up under my dad's wrath. I had been without him all my life. I spent years hoping to be with him, see him, and please him, so I could have a real relationship with him.

Over ten years I waited. Ten years! And now, what a mess I made of things. I hoped for his love. Instead, I was overwhelmed by his judgment. It was devastating.

Now, it was over. I was finished. The only thing I knew to do was leave. I mean, disappear from Montreal and disappear from my dad; just drop off the face of the earth.

I went home to my happy little apartment and packed my stuff making ready for the long, hard trip back to Edmonton. My hopes had slipped through my fingers and I'd have to make it without my father in my life once more. I was broken.

ON THE ROAD AGAIN

Monday morning came and I didn't show up for work at my dad's shop. Monday evening came and I didn't show up at the bucket factory. And when the weekend came, that company didn't see hide nor hair of me either. I walked away without a word.

I gave no notices and I picked up no paychecks. Nothing. I just vanished. Foolish? Perhaps. But I felt so destroyed, I had to get away.

I left Montreal behind and headed south to the U.S. border. I looked in my rear-view mirror several times and just like the man from the bushes, my past faded away into history. I was filled with deep, deep sorrow . . . and I cried.

I crossed the border through New York state. I preferred this route instead of facing the Canadian prairies again.

As I drove I wondered what was wrong with me. Why couldn't I be loved by anyone? Then I remembered God loved me. That helped a little but I was so depressed I found no comfort in it.

Within a few days, I had driven to Yellowstone National Park which borders parts of Idaho, Montana, and Wyoming. The park was interesting to see and I should have enjoyed it but grief stole my joy away. I felt like I had just lost my soul.

WHISPERS SAVED MY LIFE

I stopped by a "lookout" point at the Grand Canyon of the Yellowstone. I remember getting out of the car and walking toward the safety rail. Looking down upon the rocks and woods below I felt so overwhelmed by all that had happened, I thought I may as well just end it all.

I swung my legs over the guard rail designed to keep people back from the dangers below and I walked out onto the crumbling ledge. The depth of the gorge is 800-1200 feet, down to the bottom of the canyon . . . but I didn't care. My depression was so deep I wished I had the guts to push myself off.

I could hear other tourists *whispering* behind me from the safe side of the fencing. I know they were fearful for me, but again, I didn't care. Their presence did, however, stir me back to conscious reality. Thankfully no one made a move. If they had It may have caused me to fall or jump.

After a time, I made my way back to the car and continued down the road. I figured I'd go on to Edmonton as planned and try to start my life over. What else was I to do?

LOOKING FOR SUITABLE WORK

I needed a plan so I could somehow rebuild my life, but the first thing I needed was a job. I was lost, lonely, and confused. Even so, I pressed on. Thank goodness I was able to move back in with my parents. At least I had food and shelter.

I tried various occupations. First, I tried selling Kirby vacuum cleaners. I don't think I sold even one in the two weeks I worked there.

Why? Because I can't sell. I should have learned my lesson from my previous telemarketing job. But the last straw was when they wanted me to sell a vacuum to a poor, old lady in a rental house that didn't even have carpets. That's right, not a thread. They wanted me to convince her to buy the unit to clean her sofa and mattress. I was so disgusted, I quit.

I tried a couple of other avenues; I don't remember what they were but I felt like I wasn't getting anywhere.

Finally, I was so sick and tired of my sorry self that I called my dad back in Montreal and told him, "Dad, I need a psychiatrist, and by golly, you are going to pay for it because it's your fault that I'm all screwed up!" Yes, I said that to him.

To my surprise, he said "Okay," and he did pay my $600 bill. That was the first I had spoken to him since I left and there was no further discussion about where I was or if I was okay. I didn't speak to him after that for six more years.

That day, I opened the yellow pages and turned to "psychologists" and simply stabbed the page with my finger picking out whichever name I landed on.

There, I pointed to a Dr. McPherson. I called the number, and amazingly, he answered the phone, not a secretary.

In a disjointed manner, I explained I needed help and he immediately complimented me, telling me it took a lot of courage to call for support.

We set up an appointment, and that was the foundation for the next turning point in my life.

A DIFFERENT VIEW

For the next few weeks, I spent several sessions crying in front of Dr. McPherson, telling him about the hurts in my life. He was very understanding and helpful and eventually I began to believe I might have reason to live after all.

When we got through with all of that, the good doctor suggested we explore some career options. I completed a few tests including aptitude and I.Q. tests.

I don't remember what my I.Q. score was but he said I was in the 96th percentile. I thought that was pretty good since I had been told by both dads that I was *stupid.* Now I saw the possibility that they were both wrong.

As far as aptitude, the test showed I was supposed to be an architect. That was a different view, for sure. The test determined I have very abstract thinking and good perception. And I met the eleven traits, or skills, needed to succeed in the field. One of them was "organization."

I was also told I had a high aptitude for math but was nowhere near my potential because I was quite behind in my skills. The fact is, I had never achieved much in math because I was afraid of it.

Why? Because my dad used to ridicule me over it. He'd place me in a circle of adults and would grill me with math questions like times tables. Then they all laughed at me when I couldn't produce the answers. How cruel was that?

I know we have to let go of our wounds, but I was about seven when that happened, and I avoided math from then on. So now, at the age of 20, I was supposed to go back to school and catch up on all the math I missed? Right. I don't think so.

A PLAN COMES TOGETHER

The doctor said if I brushed up on my math and finished getting my G.E.D. I could then enroll in a university to study architecture. I felt as though he was teasing me with success but I wasn't buying it . . . at first.

In the days that followed, I reconsidered his suggestions. Maybe there *were* new horizons for me. It was an unexpected sort of plan but maybe it was worth a try.

Hoping I finally had direction, I enrolled in night classes so I could earn my diploma. And yes, I threw in some extra math courses, too.

I found a day job cleaning house for a wealthy couple who were both doctors. They had a huge house, two stories, with lots of tile floors to wash along with dusting, tidying, and even some sewing. The many duties required me to work there five mornings a week.

On top of that, I found a weekend job in a self-serve gas station. The owners were very nice people and had a dog that lived on the premises; a black lab named Buffy. He was great. I was a dog lover, through and through, so the setup couldn't be more perfect.

My job was quite easy. All I did was sit and process payments for gas and merchandise. The gas station was in a quiet part of town so it wasn't that busy most of the time. That left me with lots of time to study for school.

CHAPTER SEVENTEEN

GIVE ME ALL YOUR MONEY

My boss showed me how to make regular cash drops to avoid keeping large amounts in the till. We had a safe in the floor, and every hour or two I was supposed to pull all the big bills and most of the twenties, bundle them, and drop them through the slot in the floor.

But good plans only work well if you work them. I remembered to dump the cash most of the time, but sometimes I'd forget. No worries though, right? After all, what are the chances of being robbed?

One evening, while manning the gas bar, I noticed how unusually quiet it seemed. All of a sudden two men walked in and when they did, Buffy started to growl. I could always tell when he didn't like someone.

The man on the right had a knife in his hand. The man on the left had a gun. He pointed it at me and said, "Give me all your money."

I just sat there. I was shocked. Then I thought that if I did nothing, maybe someone would come along and help me. I don't know how many seconds passed but the man with the gun started getting animated. He started waving the gun around saying,

"Come on. I said give me all your money!"

Reluctantly, I opened the cash drawer and started bailing it out. I kept thinking I should have made a cash drop; I think I handed them about $600.

Regretfully, I looked at the bills as I piled them on the counter. The man with the gun snatched them up with his grubby hand, and then they were gone. It took me a few minutes to calm myself down and when I was settled enough to handle the telephone I called the police.

Officers were there in a matter of minutes and wanted to know if I was injured. I was shaken but I was alright.

Then I had to call my boss. In some ways that was harder than facing the robbers. I know they were not happy about the loss, but they were always kind to me and wanted to make sure I was okay. I assured them I was and that Buffy's presence protected me.

I didn't tell my parents about it because my mother was such a terrible worrier. But I couldn't hide it very long because my stepdad found out about it when he read it in the paper.

Later, when we were alone he questioned me and I admitted that the robbery happened. He said he wouldn't tell Mom. I was glad.

OOPS

The months went by and I continued to be faithful to do whatever was in front of me. I took care of both my jobs and my studies though I did find the math classes unpleasant. No matter what it would take to succeed I planned to finish. Then the unthinkable happened. I had a wreck.

I still had my VW Rabbit and was heading home from my house-cleaning job. I was on a four-lane road and at one point had to go down a hill to dip under an overpass. As I came up the hill on the other side my eyes were not focused high enough to see the truck stretched across the road at the top.

I was doing about 50 m.p.h. and by the time I saw him, it was too late. I had about three seconds to impact. Oops. "Bang!"

We're not talking Chevrolet here. We're talking Mack truck. He was an eighteen-wheeler with a "pup" extension. I smacked right into the side of his tire.

111

I hit it so hard, the brand name of the tire was stamped into the hood of my nice white car.

The car rolled back, the door flung open, and I rolled out onto the grass next to the road. EMTs were there in a heartbeat. They were trying to check me over but I kept moaning, "My car. My car." They said, "Never mind your car. Are *you* okay?" I was fine, sort of.

I was not wearing a seat belt so I held on tightly to the steering wheel to brace myself for the impact. The bad part of that was the force transferred from the steering wheel to my arm and cracked my wrist.

Holding on kept me from going through the windshield although I did bounce up and hit my head on the rearview mirror. I never did pass out but I was in shock for several hours. I was taken to the hospital by ambulance. By the way, back then the ride only cost fifty-six dollars. Imagine that.

Upon arrival, the doctor put a cast on my wrist and a band-aid on my forehead. Then I lay there waiting to be discharged.

Soon, a cop walked into the room. He had zero bedside manner. The first thing he said was,

"Do you know you could have been killed?"

I was silent.

"The way you hit that truck, if you had been a few feet to the left of his back wheel, the car would have jammed under the trailer and the bottom of it would have sheered off your head."

That made me angry so I kicked him out of my room. I can't remember why he stopped by. Maybe there had been some other conversation that I can't recall. Maybe he had a daughter or a sister and he was thinking of me as he would them. Or maybe he was just a nice guy trying to help. I don't know but I just couldn't take his lecture.

REALITY SET IN

My car was towed to my employer's gas station, and I later called to say I'd be at work at my usual time. They were relieved to hear my voice because when the car arrived, there was blood on the seat and the car was totaled. They told me later they both wondered if I had even survived.

I went to work at three o'clock but around eight that evening the shock wore off and I broke down into tears. I called my boss and asked him to take over so I could go home.

Being in shock is strange. It's like a protective veil that keeps you separated from your emotions but when the protective veil wears off it's like a mountain falling on you; reality sets in. Only when it hit me was I able to process in my mind what had happened.

The accident was also a wake-up call. All of life seemed to grind to a halt and I had to ask myself why on God's green earth was I studying math. Why did I want to be an architect? Really? It was a deep, soul-searching time.

Meanwhile, I had a wrecked car, insurance claims, lawyers, and transportation needs to figure out. Injured or not, there was plenty for me to do.

It turns out the doctor couple I worked for had a lawyer they referred me to. He helped me with my case and determined the semi-truck had no business being stretched out across the road like that. So the blame was placed on him and I was able to collect the value of my car.

I was sad, though, because I only had three payments left and now it was gone. My little white Rabbit was sent to the junkyard as a crushed, broken heap of scrap metal.

THE INDIAN BURNER

My friend, Darryl, sold me his old car for $300 so at least temporarily, I had something to drive. It was a 1964 Mercury and I hated it. For real. Folks used to call it an "Indian burner." I'm not sure why, but I did find a drunk Indian asleep in the back seat one day. I had a hard time getting him out of there. Anyway, the car helped me get from point A to point B so at least I wasn't walking or riding the bus.

That old car was big and ugly and it handled like a German tank. It would overheat and was sometimes hard to start. Then one of our mechanics explained that my car had a generator (not an alternator) and it wasn't working properly causing the battery to go down. Darryl seemed to know all about it, too.

I was just ambitious enough to try and fix it myself, so one Sunday, with Darryl helping me by phone, I removed the generator, took it apart, and installed new brushes (or contacts). Then I put it all back together, and "voila." I was ready to go.

Uh-h-h not so fast. I had an extra wire hanging out that needed to be attached . . . somewhere. Oh no. Now what?

So I called Darryl back and realized I would have to take the part back off and open it up again. That's when I discovered I had put one of the long screws in backward, and *that* was the screw the extra wire went to. *Sheesh.*

Thirteen hours later I got her done. One thing I learned was that I'm not a mechanic, but, the other point is that I'm hard-headed and will try almost anything. Yes, that "what if" thing was still working in me.

HAIRPIN TURN

After my accident, I quit night school. It wasn't for me. I had something else stirring deep within me, calling me in a more natural direction. It was time to make a sharp hairpin turn and get back into music. That's where my joy was.

Edmonton has the most wonderful music school in the country, housed at Grant MacEwan University and I made up my mind I was going to go there.

I still had to get my G.E.D. but I only needed three more credits. I figured that wouldn't be too hard if I buckled down and persevered.

Then I was told the credits had already been conferred toward my diploma simply due to my age. So, I had enough credits to cover what I needed.

What does that mean? It means that because of what's called "life experience" a certain number of credits are automatically added to one's record each year. They said all I had to do was apply for my high school diploma and they would issue it.

So, I applied and received my G.E.D. in the mail. Wow. What a blessing.

My next step was to audition at Grant MacEwan University's Music School. I wanted to major in drums so my audition was set up with Mr. Bob Myers.

He played for the Edmonton Symphony but sometimes he also played in Tommy Banks' band. All the teachers at the school were professional musicians.

I was hoping for a good audition but wasn't confident I'd be accepted. I was feeling unworthy but I was willing to try.

THE BIG DAY

I was sitting on a lounge chair in Mr. Myers' outer office when he opened his door and invited me in. He interviewed me to learn what my musical experiences were, and then he tested my musical aptitudes.

He started with ear training, playing some notes on the piano and asking me how far apart they were. I hadn't learned about intervals yet, but given a set of possible choices, I seemed to guess the correct answers.

He asked me some questions about chord structures, and he also tested my melodic memory. I would have to sing short melodic phrases back to him.

Next, I was tested for rhythmic memory. He clapped a pattern and asked me to clap it back. Some of the patterns were pretty complicated but I tried. I hoped I was getting it right.

At the end of the interview, I was nervous and it showed. (It was that old, "you're too dumb and you're not worth anything" syndrome.) I blurted out that I hoped to be accepted but wasn't sure because I was "just a dumb drummer." Here is what he said:

"Kathy, you are far from being a dumb drummer. You've done very well on these tests and you have a high level of musical ability, even beyond what you realize.

"Yes, *we will* accept you into our school. So in the next few weeks until the semester starts, I'm going to assign you some lessons to get you ready for classes. You need to know more about reading music and terminology. You'll also need to look over the syllabus so you can be prepared to choose your electives.

"Again, you've done well here today, and we look forward to having you as a student."

Self-esteem cannot be fixed from the outside when what is broken is on the inside. The compliment was nice at that moment, though, but it didn't help me believe in myself in the long run. That would require healing and it would come later.

When I got out of there, I cried. Imagine me, a music student in Western Canada's most prominent jazz school; a school modeled after the Berklee School of Music in the states.

Berklee College of Music was founded in Boston, Massachusetts but has sister schools in New York City and Valencia, Spain. Berklee is the largest independent college of contemporary music in the world. It is known for the study of jazz and modern American music.

All I could think was "Wow! This is the right track for me."

Years later, I wished I could have thanked God for this blessing, but I still was not walking with him.

I should mention one more thing. As I was about to start school, I realized I would be known as "Kathy Debreceni." That was quite a mouthful. When I would tell folks my last name, they'd say, "Huh?"

What if . . . I changed my name? I could do that, right? But what would I change it to? Riding along one day, I happened to notice a giant billboard. They were advertising something or other but I whizzed by too fast to get the gist of it. I did notice someone's name on it though, in big black letters. The name was, "Frost." I thought, "Say . . . that's a pretty good name"

I meditated on it for several days and started looking into how I could change my surname without a lawyer. I called various government agencies and discovered all the right steps to take. So, I proceeded forward and legally changed my name to, "Frost." (Years later, when I told my dad, he was not happy about it but it worked well for the music business.)

CHAPTER EIGHTEEN

DRUM CLASS

Looking back, I remember starting out at Grant MacEwan. I was sitting in a room with 20 other drummers. We were waiting for Mr. Myers to arrive and begin the class and it struck me that all of us were "fidgeting." Many of us were tapping our toes or bopping one knee up and down with raised heels.

I guess it's something drummers do. I was no exception. As early as grade six, I used to constantly rap on the edge of my desk with my index fingers. I drove everybody *nuts.*

In that class, we learned various groove patterns and practiced "trading fours" with sit-in musicians. The ensemble would play for several bars and then stop for four bars so the drummer could take a turn soloing.

Soloing was always stressful for me because I didn't know how to be interesting. It was good that we learned tricks and techniques to build a mental library of ideas to apply to such situations.

We also used to play as a group of drummers, using practice pads. We would read through and play rudimental drum exercises filled with flams, (where two sticks strike the pad a fraction of a second apart), paradiddles, (which are played using sticking patterns like "left, right, left, left, right, left, right, right") and rolls.

Of course, we also learned proper hand techniques like how to hold the sticks. This is very important because if you're not holding the sticks correctly, you're working against yourself and will never be able to pick up speed, control, or consistency.

I think I was the only girl enrolled in the class and back then, female drummers were rare. My interest was never based on my trying to strut my

118

gender. My interest in drums was genuine. I have a deep sense of rhythm in my being and I'm driven to express it.

I was where I was supposed to be and I learned so much more that first year than I ever dreamed. My classes included: music theory, ear training, literature and style, ensemble playing, drums/percussion, music copying, electronic music, counterpoint (harmony), form and analysis, and functional keyboard.

MY SECOND YEAR

In my second year, I wanted to continue with my drum major but the program was designed to shift the focus to vibraphones instead of the drum set. I did not want to be a vibe or mallet player so I had to switch my major to music composition.

I had already written a few songs, and now I was about to learn commercial writing skills. My second year included composition classes where I learned to create professional-sounding music.

I also learned how to compose music in all styles. We would take a song and then rewrite it as a rock song, then a country song, then a ballad, then a classical song, and so on.

All of our projects were produced in the recording studio on campus. It was awesome. The head technician's name was Clive. He was from Britain and he had the most amazing ears. Well, not his physical ears, of course. I was referring to his *hearing* ability.

Once, during a recording session, he stopped everything because he could hear air coming through the vent near the front door. I mean, the band was playing, but he could hear this whisper of air mixed in with the music. Unreal!

IT GETS TECHNICAL

One of my favorite assignments was writing a song for a big band. That exercise tested all my musical skills to date. The arrangement was for five trumpets, five trombones, five saxophones, and a rhythm section.

To complicate things, band instruments are tuned to different keys. Let me explain.

For example, the B flat clarinet plays in the key of B flat meaning that any note it plays on the staff will sound one whole step lower (because a B flat note is one whole step below C).

So, if we want a flute and a B flat clarinet to play the note, C, in unison, we will have to write a C for the flute and a D for the clarinet.

Some instruments even use different clefs--other than the bass and treble clefs--mostly to keep from having to use a lot of ledger lines, (lines outside a staff of music).

Yes, it gets technical. So when you're looking down at a score (the conductor's copy of the music showing all the instrument parts), some instruments will be in different keys.

There is such a thing as a "concert score." This type of score shows all the parts in a transposed mode so the conductor can see everything in one key and can relate to it more fluidly.

It's a lot to think about when the music is whizzing by and you hear a wrong note. Then you have to stop and figure out how you're going to communicate with the player so you can make the proper correction.

So, about my big band composition, here's the icing on the cake. I worked on my creation for a few months and imagined all the instruments playing together. I played a few sections of it on the piano for myself, but I didn't really know how it would sound.

Then the day came for me to present the song to the band. The players took their seats, the music was distributed, I counted in the tempo, "one, two, three, four," and off we went.

In the next few minutes, my ears took in everything I had written and imagined in my mind. Now, I was hearing it in the air for the first time. It was overwhelming! Not that my writing was so wonderful, but hearing what I had only imagined before was a fantastical thing.

FRIENDS

I made some wonderful friends at Grant MacEwan. Let me tell you about two of them.

I have recently been in touch with these two guys after about 40 years. They still live in Edmonton and they're still involved in music. They always wondered what happened to me as we had lost touch over the years.

I loved these guys, as friends go. In my heart, I never let them go and they never disappeared from my memory. We had good times in our five years together, playing in bands and hanging out in our spare time.

My friends, Dan and Will are twins, although they're not identical. Both are very talented, and it was a joy for me to play with them. Dan is a bass player and a vibe player. He also creates a lot of electronic music. Will is a guitar player but can play other instruments like banjo.

We played many jazz gigs back in the day. We played in restaurants, lounges, nightclubs, and other venues.

HOW I STARTED SINGING

It was Will that encouraged me to start singing. Once, he booked us into a late-night lounge but the deal was, the manager would not hire us unless we had a vocalist.

When Will came back to tell us the good news, I was flabbergasted. I looked at him in disbelief and said, "But Will. None of us sing."

He said, "I guess you will, then." And that was that.

We got busy right away, practicing in Dan and Will's living room. For two weeks, we went over songs like, *You've Got a Friend, Sunny, You are the Sunshine of My Life, It's Too Late, Yesterday,* and others.

When it was time to do the gig, we did it and everything seemed to work out just fine. And I discovered that I could sing lead and play drums at the same time. So, from that day forward, I marketed myself as a drummer/singer. And that's how I made my living for the next several years.

THE MUSIC BUSINESS

Most of our gigs were great like when we played for Mr. Shu. He owned an Asian restaurant in Edmonton and we used to set up in his front widow. I used to always sing, *How High The Moon* because he loved it and he'd always make nice comments.

We played a couple of private parties, and would sometimes bring a sax player with us or a horn player.

We played at the prestigious Petroleum Club for a while and they liked slow dancing there. I played rhythm guitar for those engagements, not drums. I would sing songs like *Autumn Leaves, It's Too Late, Sunny,* and *The Girl from Ipanema.* Dan used to snicker over everyone dancing and said it sounded like "the shuffle of the dead" out there.

We also had a long engagement at an Italian restaurant downtown. Most nights we played there from four to nine. We also entertained the Edmonton Eskimos football team (now called the Elks) at private parties there. *That* was great.

YOU'RE FIRED

The owner used to watch me play the drums and came to the conclusion that I could multitask. So he hired me to work in the kitchen during the day time. I would assist the short-order cook during the lunch rush. The rest of the time I did prep work cutting up vegetables and keeping the place clean.

I was lousy at all of it. I burned a tray of biscuits once and stunk up the whole place. Another time, I was opening a big bag of chips and it exploded. The fallout went through the window where food is passed from the kitchen to the waitresses. Chips landed on everything. Needless to say, the boss was not impressed.

After six months in the kitchen, I was fired. No hard feelings. I was still allowed to keep my band job, though.

SPREADING MY WINGS

As a musician, I was becoming more well-known and was able to freelance in Edmonton. I hooked up with all kinds of bands on a temporary basis.

I was often called at the last minute, just to cover someone who got sick or couldn't play for some reason. And there were usually no rehearsals. I'd just show up to the gig, set up my drums, and somebody would count, one, two, three, four, and we were playing.

Sometimes, they didn't even tell me what song we were about to play or what the time signature was.

I just had to figure it out. When the show was over, I was paid and went home. End of story. I was always thankful for those opportunities.

Then there were the not-so-good gigs I wasn't prepared for. Yes, it's good to stretch oneself, but there are limits.

One time I played with a band in a biker bar. We thought we had enough Rockabilly to keep them happy, but they weren't impressed. We were fired after one set.

Another time I was booked for a New Year's Eve party but we had a throw-together band and we were awful. We got fired a couple of hours into the night, before "the ball dropped." Oh well. C'est la vie! (That's life.)

I remember one other occasion when I was criticized by a bar owner because he didn't like my "bass drum technique." Really? Talk about a micro-manager. What did he know? We finished our night but never went back.

LEARNING NEW THINGS

I have had a lot of experiences. I have had to wear costumes and bang a snare drum for hours on end. At times I'd play for a meal or even for free. I've played all kinds of music from jazz to rock to country. It was a wide-open field and I worked a lot, even though I didn't make a ton of money.

I was a good player but there was still one thing I had to fix. It's called the "backbeat." It's the stroke of the snare drum that lands on beats two and four of a song in four-four time. Let me explain.

In jazz, the backbeat can be rather undefined or even missing. Jazz drumming, especially be-bop and fast swing is busy drumming. It's "messy." The left hand on the snare pops in and out, here and there in response to someone else's phrasing or as a set-up for some phrase, about to happen.

In rock and country music that backbeat is a steady and precise loud "crack." It's what "kicks" or motivates the players to put their stuff out there. Well, as a jazz-trained drummer, I didn't play with that way.

The lead-guitar player in a country band I played in took notice. Of my style. After a couple of nights, he sat me down and explained what he needed from me.

Some of the other players caught wind of it and started making fun of me. But the guitar player was trying to help. He opened my mind to a new way of hearing certain styles of music.

I listened and began correcting my shortfall. It was a valuable lesson because I improved my playing and fit in better with more bands, down the line.

I BLEW OUT MY VOICE

There was one more important thing I needed to learn: how to sing properly. Without understanding why, I *blew out my voice* after a *loud* gig one night. The next morning, I found myself waking up with a very hoarse throat. I struggled for a couple of weeks and decided I needed vocal lessons.

I had the pleasure of studying voice with Sherrill Demarco. She had had a glittering career in Opera and Broadway in New York and San Francisco.

Sherrill worked with me for three months at Alberta College. She helped me tremendously and also understood that I was a jazz/pop singer and didn't want to end up sounding *operatic* when we were done.

That training served as a foundation for the rest of my days as a singer. I will be forever grateful to her.

125

CHAPTER NINETEEN

I GOT DISCOVERED!

The next thing I knew, I was being watched. By who, you ask? Well, there was a bass player and a guitar player that had come to see our band during their break between sets; they were playing in a bar somewhere down the street.

They told me later how one elbowed the other and said, "Is that a girl on the drums?" As they got closer, they realized I *was* a girl. We soon went on our break and they wasted no time coming over to talk to me.

These boys had an offer I couldn't refuse. They had a top 40 band and they traveled all over western Canada. They needed a drummer for their three-piece band but they made it clear, there would be no slack in the workload. Everyone would need to help run the show.

We would all sing backup vocals and take turns singing lead parts, the bass player would run the lights from the stage, and the guitar player doubled on a programed keyboard and would run the sound system.

They guaranteed me $500 a week, cash, no matter what. It would be a grueling schedule, but I was twenty-three-years-old and had a lot of energy. So, I said, "Yes."

RAYDEO

The band was called Raydeo. We practiced eight hours a day for three weeks, and then we hit the road. We went to places like Fort McMurray, Hay River, Yellowknife, and a few towns in British Columbia.

We usually played Monday through Saturday and traveled on Sundays. It took us six to eight full hours to set up our equipment. I had a platform riser for my drums and a complete microphone system.

A LESSON IN RUNNING SOUND

Rick, the guitar player, used to run a "white noise check" to equalize the sound response of each room we played. This is a procedure you go through by listening to the "noise" the EQ unit sends out which guides you to eliminate feedback from your P.A. system.

You isolate each frequency (EQ) band and increase the volume until your speakers produce feedback noise. Then you pull back the gain on that frequency until the feedback stops. This process takes a bit of time but it's worth it in the long run.

Our EQ settings were always good so we rarely were troubled with feedback during shows. Even today, it bugs me when I hear feedback, and the only thing folks know to do is turn the main volume down.

I hate to bore you with this but the simple truth is if they would pay attention to the pitch of the feedback, they could pull the volume down within that EQ range and still keep a decent overall volume. So there you go. Free lesson for the day.

WE OFFERED EXCITING ENTERTAINMENT

Rick, and Dave both had wireless guitars which meant they didn't have to be plugged into the sound system with a physical wire. That was great because when the show got rolling, they would leave the stage and play from the dance floor.

Sometimes one of them would climb up on top of a speaker stack and play. Yeah, a bit showy but the people loved it. That's what they came for: to be entertained. And between the three of us, I think we did a pretty good job.

We featured all the hits of the day, hence the name "Raydeo." Just about everything you'd hear on the air we played in the clubs.

We had four nightly sets complete with costume changes and we separated each set according to the genre: rock, country, 50s, and pop. The more exciting the music, the more the cash register went "cha-ching" and in the bar-band industry, that's how success is measured. As long as the bar is making money, so are you.

THE THRILL OF IT ALL

During my time with Raydeo, we usually played from nine or ten at night until one or two in the morning. Some towns had crowds lined up at the door waiting to get in. Some bars even charged a cover fee. It was quite an experience for me. Here's part of our setlist:

Talking In Your Sleep, I'm So Excited, The Heat Is On, Every Breath You Take, Stray Cat Strut, I Saw Her Standing There, Queen Of Hearts, Jump, Footloose, Led Zepplin's Rock 'N Roll, and *Who Can It Be Now.*

People got excited over these songs, especially the song, *Jump* by Van Halen. As soon as they heard that iconic keyboard intro, they screamed and ran to the dance floor. Yes, I played hard every night. Drumming is very physical.

I used to go through about a dozen pairs of sticks a month. The cost per month was roughly eighty dollars or about a thousand dollars a year but that was the price of doing business.

I had a bag of sticks hanging on the side of my floor-tom and when they'd break I'd wing them off to the side of the stage while grabbing another one. It was one smooth motion without a hiccup. The guitar

128

player used to smile at me when I did that. I'm thankful for the skills and thrills and the memories I'll have for the rest of my life.

I HOPE THE ICE DOESN'T BREAK

My favorite place to play was Yellowknife in the Northwest Territories, (N.W.T.). This is the most populated area in northern Canada. Yellowknife is a large town, parallel to the state of Alaska. From Edmonton, Alberta, it's over 900 miles and takes 15 non-stop hours of driving time.

To get to Yellowknife, you need to cross the Mackenzie River--the second-longest river in North America.

In the summer, there's a ferry. In the winter, the river freezes over, so it's possible to drive across the ice.

However, there's a tricky period between summer and winter. For six weeks, twice a year, the ice is too thick to break up, but too thin to drive on. So the only way to get to Yellowknife is to fly.

We made the trip twice. Once in summer, and once in winter. During our summer trip, we stopped to look at some pretty waterfalls but we left our van lights on. We didn't notice until we walked back to the vehicle. God must have been on our side that day because the engine did start!

During our winter trip, we had to drive across the frozen Mackenzie River. If you've ever watched the show, *Ice Road Truckers,* you'll know what I'm talking about. Driving over frozen water is creepy, to say the least. I was praying the ice wouldn't break.

Yellowknife is a sweet town. I remember dining at the Wild Cat Cafe. The floors seemed uneven when you walked in and the ceilings were very low. All the tables had checkered, plastic tablecloths. The menu was really simple. I think I ordered a hot dog and french fries . . .

The area has mostly a native population, peppered with oil workers and truck drivers. There's not much to do up there except go to the bar. Alcohol is a serious problem in the North. I felt sorry for the locals. It's like they were trapped in an isolated community and had no way out.

NIGHTLIFE

As the night wore on, there was more drinking followed by more rowdiness among the patrons. I remember one guy getting right up on the stage in Dave's face. So, Dave gently placed his foot on the guy's chest and pushed him off. It was a four-foot drop to the dance floor. (Oh well, so much for being gentle.)

By the end of the night, things could get pretty nuts. Sometimes the girls would waggle in front of Rick and Dave and lift up their shirts. They thought they were being cute or something because they had nothing on underneath. I just rolled my eyes.

Sometimes, fights would break out. I remember one time, seeing guys throwing metal chairs around. In another place, they had a chicken-wire fence in front of the bandstand. It served as a shield, and for good reason, of course. We were glad to have it.

IS THAT A FIRE ALARM?

At first, I thought eating in restaurants was cool. I could order anything I wanted and satisfy every single tastebud. The truth is, after a while, I got sick of it. It became as monotonous as the nightlife and the endless road miles in between.

I had a brilliant idea, though. I decided to get a toaster oven and set it up in my hotel room at each stop. During the week, I could make seasoned chicken, oven-baked (pre-cooked) mac and cheese, toast, and a few other delicious home-cooked dishes.

I don't remember the town, but somewhere out there, we stopped for the week and after settling into my room I fired up my little oven, put the chicken in, and set the timer. Then I puttered around the room, gathering what I needed so I could take a quick shower while my meal cooked.

So, there I was standing under the water when I said to myself, "Is that a fire alarm I hear?"

I turned off the water and sure enough, I heard loud bells ringing out from somewhere, and then I heard sirens.

I grabbed my housecoat, opened the bathroom door, and was greeted by a room full of smoke! Good grief. My toaster oven was filling the room with billows of white, smokey clouds. I tried to open a window but wasn't having much luck.

The next thing I know, I hear pounding at my door. When I opened it, firemen came rushing in to deal with my crisis.

So, what happened? Well, I forgot to take the plastic utensils out of the bottom of the oven where I stored them for travel. They had melted over the heating element and stunk up the entire hotel.

The manager was angry, my band was angry, and I was duly scolded and emphatically warned: "No more cooking in the room!"

TIME TO MOVE ON
I loved playing with Raydeo and was with them for nine months but during that time I only had two weeks off. It was hard to keep up with the lifestyle.

I would wake up around four in the afternoon, go have breakfast, then go back to my room and practice a bit on my drum-pad set.

The show started at nine or ten and we played until one or two. After that, we'd go eat and then go back to the bar for band practice until about six in the morning.

Sunday involved tearing everything down, loading the van, and driving to the next town where we'd set up, practice, and do it all over again. Night after night, day after day, week after week. I enjoyed it but it got to be strenuous and I was getting tired of the whole thing.

It was mid-winter of 1984 when I realized I was burning out. I needed to get off the road, *now.* I wondered how they would replace me and how much notice they would need. I decided to give them three months.

Three months later, they did find a guy to take my place. Yes, a guy. He sang and played drums, and of course, he had to learn all the repertoire. He had to get accustomed to the music and blend into all the sets and costume changes.

He was hired in May of that year and I was free to resign and be on my way. The chaotic world of nightclubs, crazy hours, and going from town to town-- as if that's all there was to life--was coming to an end.

It was the constant upheaval, not the music, that I had to walk away from. Music would always be my breath and my lifeblood. It was a God-given gift. But the crazy mixed-up sleep and meal schedule was like living in another world.

Yes, God has been very good to me. I've experienced a little bit of heaven on earth. Back then, I just needed a break from it and some time to rest.

SPOILED AND BROKE

I guess I was spoiled by my previous $500-a-week salary. At that point, I didn't have much money and knew something had to give. I couldn't go on staying with folks here and there. I had to find a place to live, but I couldn't afford it. What was I to do? Well, the only thing I could do was keep playing. So, I put myself out there again in my hometown of Edmonton.

I hooked up with my friends Dan and Will; the twins I had met at Grant MacEwan. I also jumped back into freelancing with various other bands.

I particularly remember one singer/guitar player I worked with named Rod. He did a lot of Elvis stuff. He was a very strong player and could carry a whole show by himself. He hired me to embellish his presentations, so together, we began playing a variety of bars and lounges but I was barely surviving.

Rod and I took this one gig in some small town to our north. We needed the money but the catch-22 was that we were both broke and hardly had the gas to get up there.

It was winter time and we had to travel in his old, unheated school bus. When we arrived, we were told the owner was not going to pay for two separate rooms. I *did not* want to share my sleeping quarters with a guy. But we had no choice; at least there were separate beds.

We had no money for food that weekend except for about five dollars between us. So we went to the store and bought a jar of peanut butter and a loaf of bread. We didn't even have jelly to go with it. Imagine that. But we survived until we were paid.

CHAPTER TWENTY

MOVING HOME

Yes, times were tough and I was the typical "starving musician." I couldn't afford an apartment for myself so I had to move back in with my mom and stepdad.

No, they weren't thrilled, not because they didn't love me but because I had this *lifestyle*. I smoked and I drank and I stayed out until all hours of the night or morning. They were either constantly worried about me or annoyed.

I know they prayed for me a lot and asked many friends and pastors to pray and that surely was what got me through during those times. God had my number but it wasn't time yet. I had to walk this broken road just a little while longer.

RENILDA

I don't know how I met this lady, but Renilda came into my life at just the opportune time. Her son, whom she would visit, lived in Edmonton but she lived in Saskatchewan by a lake in a small town somewhere north of Saskatoon.

I can't remember exactly where it was but it was a beautiful place. I know this because after I met her she invited me to come to stay with her.

She was a warm, compassionate person. She felt sorry for me because despite my "exciting life" I was quite depressed on the inside and I think she could see that.

I had come off the road and was not earning enough money to live decently. I didn't know what I needed but I knew I needed something.

I was feeling so lost and she offered me a place to stay, a listening ear, and an open door into something I should have never touched. You see, Renilda was a "white witch."

THE DEVIL'S TRAP

For all my traveling around the world, I had no idea what a white witch was, but it sounded interesting. So without too much thought, I packed some stuff into a bag and rode out of town with her. Big mistake.

It was early spring and most of the lake was still frozen. Her house was right on the edge of it and there were only a few tourists walking around. She said traffic would pick up greatly in the summer.

Renilda was a potter and made her living selling her earthenware creations to tourists. She also read Tarot cards and had a crystal ball with which she could, supposedly, tell people their futures and advise them about how to take control of their lives. I wanted that too, because I felt *my* life was out of control.

Renilda taught me how to read Tarot cards and I did a few readings for other folks. I thought I had stumbled onto something new and helpful so I began embracing it.

LOOKING FOR INSIGHT

I would ask the cards questions about what direction I should go and what kinds of decisions I should make; (dumb move). The cards I laid out would (supposedly) either affirm things for me, positively, negatively, or vaguely. (No surprise there. What else could there be? Duh.) Then I'd have to ask more questions.

That is the whole idea behind fortune telling. People come in, ask questions, then need more answers, and have to pay more to go further. It's a pretty smooth way to make money.

135

I didn't know at the time that this practice is an abomination before God but here's a verse from the English Standard Bible. It confirms what I didn't realize about this *mess.* It was wrong and dishonest and wicked, for God said, ***"If a person turns to mediums and necromancers, whoring after them, I will set my face against that person and will cut him off from among his people,"*** (Leviticus 20:6; ESV).

I was far away from God and wasn't seeking Him for my life. Here in front of me was a kind lady who believed she was helping the world. I was glad to be in her presence and at that time, I didn't know what the Bible said.

I stayed at Renilda's beautiful lake house through the summer and into the early fall. She gave me the entire second floor of her log cabin, free of charge.

My room had a balcony that faced the lake. I enjoyed the changing moods of the water and the skies. There was no end to the way one scene transformed into another, every day. The winds, the cloud cover, the storms, and the sunshine melded into beautiful, living portraits. If only I could have seen God through that.

I had a lot of time to think but nothing was solved. My days there eventually came to an end. It was time for me to return to Edmonton with my Tarot cards, crystals, and all. Unfortunately, I still hadn't figured out what I was supposed to do.

LASKO

Who's Lasko, you ask? He was an office building manager I met in downtown Edmonton, upon my return. The old, four-story building had marble floors and a creaky elevator. It housed a lot of off-beat businesses like a new-age book store, a film production office, a free-lance writer's office, and a couple of do-it-your-selfers with music studios.

I don't remember how I was drawn to this place, but I guess it was because I needed a place to rent, cheap, and heard through the grapevine I may have some luck there. I couldn't stay with my parents anymore; I had no freedom.

At first, Lasko told me he didn't have any spaces available but then he said,

"On second thought, Yes. Come to think of it, I do have a space. It's two storage closets that were combined into one large one. We took the wall out between the two. It's roughly six feet by nine feet . . . it doesn't have a window . . . but I can let you have it for . . . say, forty dollars a month."

I said, "Yes. I'll take it." And that was that. I moved a sofa bed in, to sleep on and added a clothes rack above it. I also added a three cubic foot refrigerator and a microwave so I could "cook" if that's what you'd call it.

Then I wiggled and squirmed, and packed and compacted until I found that very necessary bit of space left to store my keyboards, guitars, drums, and my P.A system. Without a doubt, they were as important to me as my bed and my fridge. Don't ask me how I did it because I don't know. All I can say is, it worked.

THE BATHTUB

I didn't have a bathroom so I used the public restroom down the hall, and as for bathing, Lasko offered me the use of his bathtub which was in his basement apartment.

I used his tub only once and it really grossed me out. It had dirt rings and stray, black hairs and I sure didn't feel clean after dipping into that mess. Yuk.

And I was worried that he might walk in on me although he always seemed very respectful.

So Lasko's bathtub didn't work out. That meant I had to travel to my mom's house every couple of days to use her shower. I was temporarily without a car at the time so I had to ride two buses to get there.

After a couple of months of that, I discovered there was a public shower in the basement of my building. It wasn't great, but it was private and I could lock the door.

MINGLING WITH NEIGHBORS

I met a few people in the building, one of whom was Ross Campbell. He had a music studio on my floor. It was quite a large space and he invited me to come practice with his band.

As we got to know each other he learned I was living in "the closet" down the hall. So, he gave me a key to his studio and said I could use it anytime. What a blessing that was.

I used his space *a lot.* I spent a great deal of time there practicing both my vocals and my guitar skills. I could make as much noise as I wanted because I always practiced after business hours when most of the people had gone home.

Additionally, the walls were carpeted, (yes, carpeted), so there was a good sound barrier to any noise my music would create. It was just what I needed to get out of my tiny space and have somewhere to go without bothering anybody.

AND THE BEAT GOES ON

Ross was an older songwriter/guitar player. His music was in the style of New Wave Rock which was a few steps removed from standard rock and roll.

New Wave music has choppy, rhythmic guitar sounds with fast and medium tempos, and lots of keyboard sounds with a flavor similar to bands like Devo, Spandau Ballet, The Cars, The Police, or The Pretenders. These were the popular bands of that day.

Ross fit right in with this genre and had an up-and-coming song on "Much Music," the Canadian equivalent of MTV.

As we became better friends, Ross found that I could play quite well so he invited me into a professional recording session to play drums and sing backup vocals on one of the songs on his album.

After laying down the drum track for a second time, I remember the engineer paused and said, "Wow. I can't believe it. That *take* took exactly the same number of minutes and seconds as the first run-through." Then he turned to me and said, "Your timing is amazing."

At that moment I kind of felt like Barney Fife, the Deputy Sheriff from the Andy Griffith show. Remember how he used to nod and smile and act all humble? That's kind of how I acted. But it was a nice compliment and it made me feel good. I could always use that.

I COULD SING LIKE "STING"

Another band I practiced with at Ross's studio was working toward a repertoire of cover songs to play in the bars. They asked me if I would be interested in just singing for them as they already had a drummer. I agreed.

One of the songs we tackled was, *Set Them Free,* by *Sting,* which was a song I always adored. Sting was the principal songwriter, lead singer, and bass guitar player for the Police.

Later, he left his band and went solo. As a solo artist, Sting has received 17 Grammy Awards and three British Awards, plus he won Song of the Year with his hit, *Every Breath You Take.*

My band was amazed at how I could duplicate Sting's inflections to the "tee." I practiced with them for a few weeks but we never got off the ground for some reason.

During that time, the keyboard player was trying to get friendly with me. One day, he asked me to move in with him. Why? He needed someone to help him with his marijuana farm. Seriously!? But I just kept thinking of all the jail time I'd have to do if we got caught, so I declined.

TEACHING

After I left this last band I was back with the twins, Dan and Will. At least, with them, I was making *some* money. And I needed it.

They had started a new thing. They had begun teaching music in a west-end music store. Dan taught bass, and Will taught guitar. The store owner invited me to come on board so I taught drums for a while.

I didn't care for teaching because the kids didn't want to get serious and settle down to practice. All they wanted to learn were rock beats and there's much more to music than just playing rock.

CHAPTER TWENTY-ONE

NIGHTS AND DAYS

Time dragged on while I lived in my little closet. I continued reading Tarot cards for myself but my life was going into a downward spiral. Most days, I was pretty much broke and depressed, and then more depressed *because* I was broke. Trust me, it wasn't fun.

I used to go across the street to the Hudson's Bay department store. They had a grocery section in the basement and would sell expired vegetables for pennies on the dollar. Most of the time I would buy a bag full to take home and steam in my microwave.

I also ate a lot of Ramen Noodles and macaroni and cheese. I washed all my dishes in the restroom down the hall. No, it wasn't like living and eating at the Hilton Garden Inn in downtown Edmonton but I was surviving.

Slowly, I got into the habit of staying up all night and sleeping through the day. It worked well because at night the building was quiet. I would sit on the cold, marble floor in the hall, rolling cigarettes with Drum brand tobacco which came in a little drawstring pouch. Tobacco and "rolly" papers were cheaper than tailor-made smokes but they were nasty smelling and strong.

Once in a while, I'd pick up a small labor job during the day just to have some extra money. Lasko asked me to paint an office for him one time but I did a really poor job. Painting is not a skill I possess.

I also did some filing for the film producer on my floor. It was a ridiculous job. He would hand me a piece of paper and tell me which file folder to put it in.

We worked like that for three or four hours until his desk was clear. I guess he just needed motivation; he couldn't do it by himself.

LIFE GOES ON

Thankfully, I did get another car because I had to have a way to haul my drums. I still played here and there with this band and that band; whatever was available.

Many nights I wouldn't get back to my building until two or three in the morning. I wondered if I would be safe, out on the city streets after the bars closed.

Loading and unloading was a chore. I had to make several trips from my little closet to the elevator which took me to the main floor. Then I had to drag my stuff from the elevator, out the front doors, and to the car. Coming home, my stuff had to be hauled back upstairs and put away.

Besides unloading all my gear on a lonely, downtown street with no one around, I later had to go and park my car in the dark alley behind the building. I was always looking over my shoulder. I didn't realize how much God was protecting me from harm in those days, but He was.

THE AXLE BLEW OUT

So, my next car was a 1971 Dodge Polara, and it was as big as a boat. It was okay to drive but it did have a problem with overheating. Getting stuck in any sort of traffic was not something I wanted to do. During the time I owned it, I only had one major repair to make on that car but it was kind of my fault.

I went to this gig one night and the bass player forgot his bass! I wondered how he could do that but, oh well, I loved the guy anyway. I mean, he was a

142

band member and my friend so I offered to go get his "axe" for him. (That's what guitar players call their instrument.)

I raced up to his condo which was a long distance north from downtown. On the way back, I was clipping along in the right lane when I realized my lane was going to disappear into a turn-only lane.

I decided to shift over into the center lane but I didn't see the triangular median in between. It was a concrete island about five inches high.

Suddenly, I hit it with my right front end, doing forty miles per hour. I heard a big *bam, screeeech, and thump.* It tore out the right wheel and broke the axle; there was other damage, too. I was amazed at how quickly it happened.

I don't remember how I left that mess but I do remember getting into a cab with my friend's guitar so I could get to the gig. I guess I must have had the car towed to a shop the next day for repairs.

After that, I sold the car to a guy who was moving to Toronto. I told him about the overheating problem so he was well warned. But he called me a couple of weeks later to tell me he was stuck in heavy traffic on the 401, Kings Highway.

The highway stretches 514 miles from Windsor to the Ontario/Quebec border. The 401, where it passes through Toronto is North America's busiest highway, and one of the widest.

I felt sorry for him but Toronto was far away from me and I had been honest with him; he knew what he was buying and I felt no responsibility. I had to remind him, "I told you it would do that."

And he very simply said, "I know." Anyway, that was the end of my Dodge.

HOPE WAS DISAPPEARING

I can report that I did get yet another vehicle for me and my drums. Later on, I will tell you how my Honda became famous. Anyway, it was a dark green, rusty 1977 Honda, Civic. I came to love that little car. I didn't know it, but one day it would carry me far, far away.

That car was the only bright spot in my life. Everything else was growing darker and darker. My paid gigs were becoming fewer, my money was low, and my hope for life was disappearing.

I thought the "guidance" from the Tarot cards would bring happiness and success into my life. But no matter what the cards said, I was discouraged.

I wasn't working much and I had given up trying. I would sleep the day away in my dark, windowless closet while the offices around me housed busy people, hard at work.

At night, I wandered the halls or listened to the bands practicing from the cold, dusty stairway. Sometimes they were so loud, I had to escape to the basement. But sometimes, there was a band down there, too. They played so loud that when I was in the shower, I could barely hear the water run.

The last thing I thought about was God. I had met him and experienced salvation almost twelve years earlier, but He was nowhere in my mind, now. It didn't occur to me that He was still there.

I MADE A NEW FRIEND

One afternoon, I slipped out to use the restroom. When I returned, the woman in the office next door to my closet had come out for a break.

She saw me and said hello. She introduced herself as Susan and said she was employed by the government to write their internal publications.

She had red hair and distinct features. She was kind of jittery and saw that I noticed; she said it was because she drank too much coffee. I, too, was kind of awkward and soon parted with her and went back to my space.

Over the next few weeks, I bumped into Susan several times. She was always kind and didn't pry into my circumstances. Yet eventually, we got around to some serious conversation.

I admitted to her that my spot next door to her office was my residence. She didn't act surprised; she just accepted it. I also found myself sharing my interest in the occult with her. She didn't judge or condemn me. She let me explain my attraction to it and how I was looking for answers for my life. She just listened.

A few more weeks went by. We continued our conversations and then at one point she told me she was a Christian. That sort of struck a nerve with me. I had been down that road but walked away from God at the age of 15. I wasn't interested in the Christian life anymore.

Then, she gave me a book. She said it was all about the occult but she warned me that it was written from a Christian perspective. The book was called, *The Beautiful Side of Evil,* by Johanna Michaelsen. Susan asked me if I'd be willing to read it and I agreed I would.

EXPLORING "JOHANNA'S" JOURNEY

Written in 1982, the back cover says, *"The last fifteen years have witnessed an explosion of interest in psychic phenomena . . . that is unprecedented in history . . .*

"This is a true account of a young woman who, while in search of spiritual truth, became a personal

assistant to a psychic surgeon in Mexico for 14 months.

"Then, in answer to her prayers, God revealed the true source behind the miraculous healings she witnessed. Lifting the veil of deception He allowed her to see the evil behind the outward appearance of beauty and holiness.

"Johanna Michaelsen reveals how this deadly deception is not isolated to her unusual experience but rather is invading our everyday lives, even in our churches."

(Purchase at: https://tinyurl.com/2mhgpxcq)

I'm not sure how closely I read the back cover. I knew the subject of "God" would come up in the book, but I was still drawn to read it; I thought I might learn something from Johanna's journey into the occult.

Her story fascinated me. It was so interesting to read how people were healed. I should mention, the book was endorsed by Hal Lindsey, a reputable and long-standing evangelist and author, famous for the book, *The Late Great Planet Earth*, released in 1971.

In Johanna's book, this so-called surgeon she worked with didn't use instruments or tools. She would just supernaturally reach into people's bodies with her hands and touch or pull out diseased organs. When the procedure was complete, the opening would magically close without a trace or a scar.

Johanna believed she was doing a good service for mankind. After all, this was "white magic" not "black magic." That's also what Renilda used to tell me. It was all done in the name of helping people.

I guess it took me a couple of weeks to read and digest the book. And right up until the last chapter, it had opened wide, the door into the world of the supernatural. Then the story changed.

The first couple of paragraphs at the end of the book signaled that I was about to hear from God. But did I want to? Not really, but I kept reading.

TRUTH SPEAKS

The final chapter uncovered the true source behind these healing powers. It was Satan. Really? How did she know? Where was the proof? Here's what Johanna had to say about God's word on the matter: [Pages 195-206.]

"We have been commanded to test the spirits. Very well. But just exactly how do we do that? How can we be certain a healing or a miracle is from God? How can we be sure our gifts are from the Lord?. . .

"1. What does he [the healer] believe about Jesus? Does he cling to Jesus Christ of Nazareth as God the Son, the second person of the trinity, God incarnate in human flesh . . . who died upon the cross in our place for the forgiveness of our sins; the one born of a virgin whose physical resurrection from the dead proclaimed His victory over sin, death, and Satan?. . .

"2. They must be one hundred percent accurate [in their works or prophecies] one hundred percent of the time . . .

"3. If a miracle or sign or prophecy or healing is performed by an occultist, or by means of occultic technique, it is counterfeit . . .

*"4. The test of the fruit of [their] life must also be applied . . . **'You will know them by their fruits,'** (Matthew 7:16; NKJV). The Lord then goes to great lengths to explain . . . that a good tree cannot produce bad fruit . . .*

*"5. The final test is that of our subjective inner witness . . . The Lord [Jesus] said, **'If any man is***

willing to do His [*God's] will, he shall know of the teaching, whether it is of God, or whether I speak from Myself,' *(John 7:17; NASB; [*word added]). If we truly want to know the Truth and are willing to be obedient to it, God will make it evident within us.*

"Understand then, before anything else, that apart from Jesus there is no hope for you. ***'And there is salvation in no one else, for there is no other name under heaven given among men by which we must be saved,'*** *(Acts 4:12; ESV). Unless you are prepared to commit your life, your body, mind, and spirit, to His Lordship, you will never find the peace and freedom you seek."*

After offering the plan of salvation, Johanna goes on to lead the reader through the prayer of renunciation, stopping all occultic activity, destroying occultic objects, applying the blood of the Lamb, putting on God's armor, and standing on His Word of truth in every area of our lives.

I slapped the book shut and just lay there. Deep inside my heart was the start of a wrestling match with myself and with God.

Why would I want to go back to that goody-two-shoes life? There would be so many restrictions. I would just be subject to a bunch of rules and regulations. And I'd have to tell folks I was a God-follower and they'd laugh at me. Did I really want to start *that* all over again?

I also knew I was deeply depressed. I had lost interest in living. There were nights when I would sit on the cold floor in my building, smoking my homemade cigarettes, trying to think up ways to end my own life.

CHAPTER TWENTY-TWO

A WRESTLING MATCH

Suicide was something I began to entertain. If I could find a gun I could shoot myself. But could I do it? I mean, really do it? I could drive my car into a bridge abutment. But what if I didn't die?

I thought about taking a drug overdose. At least that would be peaceful. I would go to sleep and never wake up. That seemed the best choice . . . so when would I do it? Hopefully soon, I thought.

I wrestled with everything for about two weeks, there in the darkness of my room. I had no answers. I was at a complete loss with nowhere to turn. I didn't want to turn to God because I knew I'd have to surrender my life completely into His control. But here I was at the end of the road. I had tried to run my life *my way* and I made a total mess of it.

KATHY, ARE YOU READY?

At that point, I don't remember if it was night or day, or what day of the week it was. My waking and sleeping hours were upside down and all the days had run together. But there, in the stillness, I heard a voice in my spirit. It wasn't audible, yet it was very clear.

God spoke to me and said, "Kathy, are you ready to follow me now?"

From the depths of my soul, the only answer I had was, "Yes, Lord."

I knew it would cost me everything. I knew I'd have to change my ways. But in the middle of my tears, I knew it was the only way. There was hope now. God was still there . . . for me! He hadn't let go of me even though I had let go of Him.

My mind was swirling. What should I do next? What was the plan? Well, whatever it was, I was not going to orchestrate it. So I continued to lay there and after an unknown amount of time, I pulled myself together.

During those two weeks of isolation, I didn't want to see anyone or talk to anyone. I just needed to figure out my next move.

When I got my bearings, I realized Sunday was approaching. I thought it might be good to go to church and reach out for help.

I didn't want to go Sunday morning; there were too many people there. Besides, I didn't want to run into Susan just yet. That's where she attended: Central Pentecostal Tabernacle. So, I went Sunday night instead. The service started at six o'clock.

REACHING OUT

I arrived a few minutes late so I could slip in the back. I made my way to the second-floor balcony and sat in the back row. I don't remember the music or the sermon. All I knew was that I needed help.

When the service was over and most of the people had shuffled out, I went down to the main floor and approached the altar area. A man (whom I later learned was the Pastor) came over to me and said, "Can I help you?"

I burst into tears. I said, "I've been running from God for 12 years and I have just decided to come back to Him. I don't know what to do, but I'm involved in a bunch of stuff that's not right, and it's ruining my life."

I explained my occult practices, the Tarot cards, the New Age teachings, the fortune telling using crystals, my seeking psychic mediums, and so forth.

I told him the whole story in between sobs. He was very tuned into what I was saying. Meanwhile, as

I stood there speaking, I could hear loud voices in my head. In my mind, they were screaming at the Pastor, saying, "You ugly, rotten piece of flesh. You're not going to help me. No. I'm going to throw up on you, right now!"

It was all so horrible, but I pressed through it.

Then the Pastor said, "Would you be willing to come to one of our back meeting rooms so several of us can pray with you?"

I nodded in agreement as he gathered five or six other men and women and we all headed behind the platform.

That's where I sat for the next three hours! Nobody cared what time it was. They just wanted to minister to me.

TIME FOR DELIVERANCE

Not many churches offer a deliverance ministry. I'd venture to say most Christians don't even know what it is or that it's necessary and vital.

Some Scriptures come to mind.

"Stay alert! Watch out for your great enemy, the devil. He prowls around like a roaring lion, looking for someone to devour," (I Peter 5:8; NLT).

*"The thief [*Satan] does not come except to steal, and to kill, and to destroy. I [*Jesus] have come that they may have life, and that they may have it more abundantly,"* (John 10:10; NKJV; [*words added]).

The devil hates Christians. He is after them at every turn. Whenever we open a door into his territory, he puts his foot in it and comes right in.

We can open doors in many ways. For example, through drugs, excessive alcohol, sex outside of marriage, false religions, New Age teachings, occult practices, and even through disasters like storms, earthquakes, and trauma like rape or brutal assaults. The devil can gain a foothold in numerous ways. It takes "deliverance" to kick the devil back out.

The people at the church were very aware of my situation. For hours they prayed as I cried and wailed and rocked back and forth in my chair. I don't remember if I threw up but they kept a waste basket nearby. They read Scriptures over me that *legally* put Satan on the run.

This kind of fight is like being in a court of law. When I, the defendant show up and the enemy shows up, my lawyers and advocates open the books and state God's word before the court to render the devil's lies powerless.

Based on God's word, as a Christian believer, I have the right to be free. But it's a battle that must be fought and won because otherwise, Satan will not leave.

ONE MORE THING

When the prayers were over, the Pastor said there was still something else I needed to do. He said I should gather up all my occult paraphernalia, the books, cards, and trinkets, and bring them back to the church.

They would arrange to have a barrel set outside when I came Wednesday night, and together we would burn it all. I had to renounce and disconnect myself from everything I had been involved in so I could properly start on my road to freedom.

I agreed and came back in three days and all that was discussed was carried out. From that time forward, I attended church regularly. In the meantime, I shared my conversion with Susan. She was elated to hear the news.

MY FAITH IN GOD WAS RENEWED

You must understand: a person cannot be saved twice. I was saved once but I fell away. As you know, I walked away from God and did not consider Him in any way for 12 years. During that time, *I* was the lord of my life. But during this Easter season of 1987, I gave my heart to Jesus, anew. And except for a few mistakes, I never looked back. I have stayed the course to the best of my ability.

As for deliverance, the devil doesn't give up easily. The prayers in the back room of the church that night were a one-time deal. But further help was needed. I was referred to a couple who practiced deliverance ministries out of their home. I believe I met with them for about six weeks.

I was still having issues with voices in my head, and a severe inability to concentrate. Through learning Scriptures and repeating them out loud during the day as needed, those symptoms faded.

I was almost free but still felt a stronghold working against me that I couldn't put my finger on. Somehow, through a friend I think, I found a Christian psychologist and author, Mr. Stan Wilson, who specialized in deliverance.

He and his partner worked with me for about a year. There was also much counseling that took place to help me with my emotional hurts and wounds. Following the counseling sessions, his partner came on board; he had a "gift of discernment." Together, they prayed over me and identified the last of those wicked spirits that were aggravating my life.

THE BATTLE IS REAL

Some people may have a hard time understanding or believing all of this. I assure you it is real. There are many Christians who need deliverance.

They find themselves hindered in their Christian walk but they have no idea why, and they have no one to talk to about it.

I was so appreciative of how God ministered to me through these helpers that I thought maybe I should go into a deliverance ministry, myself. Dr. Wilson warned me against it unless I was sure God was calling me to do so. I never felt "called" so I never ventured down that road.

Now that my faith in God was restored, I was ready to start fresh, turn a new page, and embark on whatever God had in store. And it would prove to be a most interesting ride, as you shall see.

MY BAD HABITS

Yes, I was changing in a good way but God still had a lot of work to do fixing and cleaning me up. I still had some stuff in my life that had to go.

The first change I made was to stop drinking. I just quit; walked away. It wasn't hard to do because I was never addicted to alcohol. I didn't *need* it as a few of my friends did.

Smoking was a whole other story. I truly did not want to smoke anymore but I couldn't let go of it. I tried and failed and tried and failed. It was no good.

I remember sitting cross-legged on the floor one day. I was rolling a cigarette and crying at the same time. I prayed, "God, I want to quit smoking but I can't. I don't have the willpower. It's like a ball and chain I drag around every waking hour. Will You help me?"

There was no reply, and no help seem to come. A couple of weeks later I heard about a church revival meeting at an auditorium near my house. It sounded like a good thing to attend, so I went.

I don't remember much about the music but the minister was on fire! At the end of the service, he said, "Some of you tonight are struggling with an addiction to cigarettes. God knows who you are. I want to pray for you. So all of you wanting special prayer, raise your hand."

My arm shot up like a cannonball. Then he said, "Those of you that raised your hand, I want you to come down onto this platform right now and I'm going to pray. Quickly, now. Come and receive the healing of the Lord."

I stood up and made my way down to the front. I didn't care who saw me or what people were thinking. I needed help.

The minister prayed a simple prayer of healing and deliverance from smoking. Then he dismissed us and the service ended.

I made my way out of the venue and began my walk home. I regret saying this, but at the time, I wondered if the prayer would work. I hoped it would but I didn't dwell on my doubts for too long. I just went about my business in the coming days.

God is so good. He was not dissuaded by a new believer's moment of unbelief. Because of His compassionate grace and mercy, He *did* help me. He *did* remove my addiction. He *did* heal me and deliver me and I never desired or craved another cigarette, *ever again*. Praise God; praise His mighty name.

CHAPTER TWENTY-THREE

MOVING ON UP AND MOVING OUT

A second matter of business was that God wanted me out of the bars. For a while, I thought maybe I could continue there and be a witness for Jesus. Maybe some folks are called to do that, but I wasn't.

The time came for me to go to my last rehearsal. We had practiced for an hour or so when the guys wanted to take a break. As they sat, passing around a joint, I felt an urging in my spirit. I knew what I had to say. It was a moment I had always been afraid of because I was afraid of being ridiculed.

But this was part of the price I had to pay. So while they were seated, I stood up and said, "Boys . . . I'm sorry to have to say this, but I'm getting out of the music business. Today will be my last rehearsal with you. I'll play the gig we have coming up but after that, I'm done. The reason I've decided to do this is . . . I gave my life to Jesus Christ."

The guitar player laughed, making a chortling sound through his nose. The others kind of nodded in wonderment.

So there it was. I stood up for Jesus, come what may. And I didn't care what they thought. Nothing more was said, and when my final day came, I bid everyone goodbye and I *walked*. It was time to move on to new things.

Meanwhile, Susan felt sorry for me living in that closet. I had been there for 13 months. I finally moved out and went to share her two-bedroom apartment with her. But the deal was, I had to get a job.

We talked it over and concluded what I needed was to upgrade my skill set. I needed a better work environment other than gas stations and convenience stores.

THE GRANNY DRESSES

Big changes were on the way. They affected my future employment and they affected my personal habits, too. I was *all in* with Jesus and I wanted to do everything I could to please Him. So I developed the notion, somehow, to change my entire way of dress.

I stopped wearing pants, even blue jeans, and traded them for "granny dresses." I stopped wearing make-up and jewelry, I let my hair grow straight and long, and I took on a very plain, drab appearance. To me, it wasn't about legalism. It was about being *totally* surrendered.

During that time, I had rubbed shoulders with one of the young women at church and I admired her. She had pretty, blonde hair, nice clothes, nice make-up, and bold jewelry. Somehow, I didn't think her manner of dress displeased God, yet I thought mine did. That's why my transformation was so drastic.

We chatted now and then, exchanging pleasantries. Then, she got a hold of me one day for a serious conversation. There was a quiet spirit about her and I liked that, too. She was the perfect person to ask me about my attire.

MY BARN NEEDED PAINT

She said, "Kathy, I sense in my spirit that you are troubled. Are you feeling depressed in any way?"

"No," I answered.

"I guess you're wondering why I'm asking. I'm just concerned about you. You've changed quite a bit since you first got here and mostly, I see it's been a good thing . . ."

"You see something that's not good?" I interrupted.

"Well, I don't mean *not good*, really, but . . . okay, I'll just tell you what I see, and please know I mean no offense . . . but you have become kind of plain. Your long dresses and your simple sort of appearance . . . well you seem to be avoiding anything stylish . . . with any flair . . . and I think you're robbing yourself."

"Oh . . . well . . . since I've come back to Jesus, I've wanted to please Him in every possible way. I thought my clothes, make-up, and hairstyle were offending Him. I told God I was willing to give up *everything* to follow Him . . . and . . ."

"Kathy, what you're describing is a legalistic religion and God is not the author of that. God is not asking that of you. You're allowed to be yourself. You get to stand tall and be confident and fix yourself in a way that's attractive and yet modest. God is not against beautiful things."

I had to admit, "my barn needed paint." And this girl was giving me permission to do just that. Looking around at other women in church, everyone dressed nicely and it was time for me to understand it was okay for me to do the same.

I appreciated the encouragement I received from this girl. She helped me see the pendulum didn't have to swing out quite that far.

Slowly, I found my way; I found my style and I wasn't guilty about it. God was not angry with me for abandoning my granny dresses. I didn't need them to be right with Him.

SEEKING MY FATHER

There was another matter haunting me: I had turned my back on my father, leaving on bad terms.

Six years had passed since we spoke. He told me he would never "bend his knee" to me. But whether he reached out to me or not, I felt I needed to reach out to him.

At that point, it didn't matter who was right and who was wrong. As a Christian, I believed I needed to go to him and apologize and ask for his forgiveness. And that's just what I did.

I handled the situation by telephone. I don't remember the details but I do remember that he received me and was willing to meet me halfway to bridge the gap.

Then, he surprised me by making a trip to Edmonton. He wanted to get together with me and my mother and stepdad, of all things. We spent the day at West Edmonton Mall, a huge place with every amenity you can think of. We took pictures and had a meal and walked around. It was a wonderful time of reunion. The next day, he flew home.

Ever since that day, I went to visit my dad every year. He always flew me to Montreal at his expense which was very helpful because otherwise, I wouldn't have afforded it. And he always gave me a little spending money so my sister and I could go out on the town to movies, concerts, and festivals, and have lovely meals together.

My sister and I visited the Montreal Jazz Festival several times. I have always held on to my jazz roots and she enjoyed being introduced to the genre. Years earlier I shared some of my favorite pop music with her like Supertramp and Pink Floyd. She says I really opened up a special world for her and she has appreciated music ever since.

SHARING MY TESTIMONY

During my visits home I spent a lot of time with Dad in his living room. We watched a lot of T.V. and I was glad to be with him even though we didn't talk much.

Sometimes my dad would take me fishing with him. A couple of times we even went into Montreal to look at some of the places we used to live. I loved doing that. I was so glad my relationship with my dad was restored.

If it hadn't been for Jesus in my heart I may have never tried to make things better. As we got reacquainted, my dad did notice a change in me. My language was clean and I didn't have that bad lifestyle anymore.

I shared my complete testimony with him two or three times. He didn't quite understand it but he couldn't deny that I was different. At least the seeds of the Gospel were planted and I continued to water them on many occasions over the years.

OUR FRIEND, LISA

I was beginning to grow in my Christian walk. As for church, I was there every time the doors were open. It is often said that the church is not a museum of Saints but a hospital for Sinners. It should follow that everyone is welcome to enter and bring their burdens to the Lord for healing and forgiveness.

I was one of those sinners that came through the church doors, but there were many others from all walks of life.

Susan and I became friendly with a young girl at church who I will call Lisa. Lisa was about 23 years old and lived by herself in an apartment close by. We visited her a few times and extended our hand of fellowship to her.

In time, we learned that she had a certain disability. She didn't work but instead collected a type of S.S.I. or government, supplemental income. That's because Lisa was schizophrenic.

She loved the Lord, Jesus, and she seemed to function and behave sort of normally but she did have a few strange ideas.

She would get paranoid sometimes over the oddest things. She worried that people were watching her and believed her necessary medicines--that helped curb her disease--were harmful.

ONE SCARY NIGHT!

For some reason, we invited Lisa to stay overnight with us once. Maybe we had a late dinner and then watched a movie or something; I don't remember. And unknown to us, she had abandoned her meds about three weeks before her visit.

At around midnight, Susan and I were asleep in our bedrooms; each of us had our door shut. Suddenly, Lisa burst into my room with a knife in her hand. She was completely out of her mind.

I hollered as I tried to grab her arms, holding them away from me. Susan heard me and came running from her room and the two of us struggled hard to restrain Lisa and get her off me.

There wasn't much more sleep to be had that night. Susan and I did take shifts to be on guard so each of us might catch a few more winks. But when the sun came up, we reached out to the local mental hospital.

We were able to calm Lisa down, talking to her softly and quieting her state of mind so we could deliver her to Alberta Hospital Edmonton by 6:00 AM.

Lisa remained at Alberta Hospital for three weeks while they helped stabilize her and get her back on her regular medication. She was then released to go home to her apartment.

We started seeing her back in church after that. We were still friendly with her, but we never did invite her over anymore. That was one scary night and we never wanted to go through *that* again.

NEW HORIZONS BUT FIRST, ONE MORE TASK

Everything in my life was brand new. I opened myself to new experiences and new ideas and asked God to help me at every turn. In my search for future employment or schooling, I learned of a secretarial school downtown. They needed six thousand dollars for a six-month course. That was a lot of cash for someone who was broke.

If I qualified, I could get a student loan. Upon graduation, they would do their best to place me in a job and I'd be able to pay back the loan.

Susan thought it was a good plan, but the whole thing hinged on whether I could do it. She was willing to take the risk so I jumped in with both feet.

I did qualify for a school loan that would cover my rent and living expenses during my time of study. So, with the application in hand, I was ready to sign on the dotted line and get started.

I was accepted but school was not going to start for a few months. That gave me some time to finish up one more task from my music school days.

You see, I didn't graduate because I dropped out before I could complete my final assignment. I was supposed to compose, produce, and direct a one-hour concert (recital) for the public, featuring my various compositions.

I had to cover every style of music from jazz to rock to country to classical to electronic to atonal.

(Atonal music has no key signature and does not follow any of the standard rules of music; it is indeed, very strange.)

I regretted dropping out of my program at Grant MacEwan. I didn't want things to turn out the way they had when I abandoned high school. Here was my chance to *finish* something and get my diploma.

CHAPTER TWENTY-FOUR

IT WAS A "REALLY BIG SHOW"

I had started working on my final recital before I dropped out. Now, I was coming back to complete it. Altogether, I spent a whole year creating it.

I was down to the last two months before the presentation. They said I could use anyone in the school; the students were at my disposal to play or sing in groups of any size. I would guess my cast numbered close to 100 people. It was a lot to organize.

My opening song was an arrangement written for a big band consisting of 22 guys. I also used an eight-piece, acapella choir, a woodwind duet, about a 12-piece group for my atonal selection, a jazz rhythm section (with me on guitar), and a troupe of modern dancers, somewhere in the middle of the show.

I also had a set director and half a dozen stagehands who seamlessly changed the platform between songs and curtain closings. Then there were sound and lighting staff.

The whole show was smooth from start to finish. There was no dead air or downtime; it was quite an accomplishment.

Susan came to see it, as did my parents. My peers and most of my professors were there, too. The auditorium was packed. When all was said and done I received my diploma in music composition with a minor in drums.

LETTING GO OF THE OLD

When I finished at Grant MacEwan University, I started selling off all my equipment. I sold my drums to a Christian college for $1800. I sold my P.A. system and my keyboards and anything else I had of value (except my electric guitar). I had raised enough money to catch up on my living expenses until secretarial school started.

Again, I told the Lord I was giving up *everything*. You see when I do something, I don't do it halfway. I was walking with Jesus *all the way*. Since I'd made such a mess of running my own life, it was time to turn my all, over to Him.

So, I quit music completely. I told God it was okay if He never let me have it back. I gave Him my whole heart and didn't hold anything back, even if it was dear to me.

ANOTHER MEMORABLE FIRST DAY AT SCHOOL

It was the Fall of 1988. I was looking forward to business college and looked forward to my first day of classes. While I didn't wet my pants like I had the first day of kindergarten, I did sort of make a spectacle of myself. I wasn't quite sure how to dress. I didn't want to wear "church attire" so I wore my usual spandex pants and spiked my hair like I did when I played the bars.

When I joined the other girls on that first day, I noticed they were all nicely groomed, their hair was modestly styled, and they wore dress slacks and nice tops. Whoops. Uh, I guess I sort of didn't fit in. No one said anything but I knew I needed to do better in this new world I found myself in.

I figured things out pretty quickly and then got down to the task of learning how to type, file, write business letters, and get a handle on grammar. By the way, my score on my very first typing test was negative twenty-five words per minute! (Lol.)

Classes went from nine to five, five days a week. Halfway through the course, we started thinking about what kind of office we wanted to work in, be it a medical office, a travel office, a law office, or a business office.

I added a month to my course so I could study computers. Word Perfect version 3.0 was popular at the time and I loved working with it. I chose the business environment for my workplace of choice. I looked forward to finding a job soon so I could have some money in my pocket again.

THE NEXT FOUR YEARS

I graduated once again and was looking forward to job placement. I believe the only interview I went to was at Sun Life Insurance of Canada.

This was it! I was now ready to impress someone with my grades and ambitions hoping I would get hired. I already learned that I would need to "dress the part;" dress for success you might say.

My funds were scarce so I went to a downtown consignment shop and found the absolute crispiest, navy-blue skirt and blazer with a sharp, white blouse. It was perfect.

Later that week, I went for my interview. When it was my turn to go in, a door opened and a slender older woman came out and called my name. She looked a bit like Barbara Corcoran from Shark Tank.

I was nervous but I didn't over-talk. I just replied to her questions and acted confident. In a few days, I was told I got the job. What a good break that was.

My position in the company was at the "end of their assembly line" of operations. After the insurance applications were received and input into the system and after the underwriters approved coverages and limitations, I was the last stop before the policy went out the door to the customer. I worked in a team of about a dozen women. My title was "Policy Issue Clerk."

It was a tough, high-pressure job. I had to maintain an accuracy score of above 85% or I'd be fired. I was more exhausted each night from working there than I ever was at the car wash or the post office. It was grueling.

CHANGE WAS NEEDED

I stayed at Sun Life for a full two years. My annual salary was $26,000 by the time I left. Not bad for the late 80s. But the money couldn't keep me there any longer. I gave my notice and left the job without any future prospects. At least I was a trained secretary now; I was sure I would find something else.

I made another change in my life just a few months before leaving my job. I changed churches.

God started talking to me about leaving Central Pentecostal and going to Beulah Alliance Church. My parents and I went there years ago when we were first saved.

I argued with God, "But Lord, I don't want to leave Central. The music is great, the preaching is great, the people are great . . . why would I want to leave?"

But God kept bringing it to my mind in a gentle way. He kept urging me to go one Sunday and just try it.

The Sunday in question came. I drove to this other part of town, to Beulah's old building; they were building a new church at the time. I found a spot to sit five or six rows from the front and took in the service.

The Pastor, Albert Runge, was a messianic Jew. I loved him. His words and the whole atmosphere brought a tangible presence of God into the sanctuary. The music was good, too. They had a very large choir and a small orchestra.

All I can say is that I was drawn to go back. And I continued there until I joined and became a member.

So why is this important? Because God takes our lives and weaves into them the most amazing tapestry. At this point, all I saw was the underside of the needlework; the tied, knotted threads, and the undefined picture, but later I realized the sheer art that was being created on the other side. You will see it too, as this story keeps unfolding.

THE MUSIC DIRECTOR

I had been attending Beulah for a couple of months when the music director, Steve, singled me out one day after service and said, "A little bird told me that you can sing."

I didn't know what to say. I downplayed any musical talent I might have had and told him I wasn't involved in music anymore. He asked me why and I simply said I had given it all up and given it over to the Lord.

He said, "Did you ever think that maybe God is calling you back to it?"

His words hung in the air like flowers suspended from a basket. I just shrugged and said I'd think about it. I didn't want to do anything against God. I had given up music three years ago and I was prepared to give it up forever. But is that what God wanted for me in the long term? I'd have to pray and ask Him.

As I spent time in prayer, I felt God's peace. That's one way to know, as a Christian, that we are going in the right direction. When we go against God's will, our spirit becomes troubled. When we follow God's plan He gives us the peace that passes understanding. It's profound.

I felt God leading me to get involved in music once again. But it would be different this time. It would be music that glorified Him in a house of worship. When I understood that, I went back to Steve and told him I was ready to join the choir.

I WAS RESTORED

God is in the "restoration" business. He takes the lives of people who are broken and He makes them whole again. It usually doesn't happen all at once. It's a process. As long as we continue to surrender our hearts, He can work with us and mold us into who we were created to be.

Some folks don't want to accept Christ because they're afraid they'll lose themselves; that they won't be authentic anymore; that they will have to give up their power and control at every turn.

Nothing could be further from the truth. Yes, we do have to give up control but the result will be something so much better. When we surrender to God, He shapes us into the being for which He intended. That's when we find our *real* identity.

It's like this: suppose you were created to be a cherry tree. But growing up, you dream about being a pine tree. You admire pine trees. You love producing the cones that carpet the forest floor in the Fall and from them, many new pine trees grow. You love having strong branches upon which to invite squirrels to come and play, to race and swirl from bottom to top, as they scurry to neighboring trees and back again.

But then you get a glimpse of God's intent for you and you surrender. Pretty soon you're filled with beautiful white blossoms. After that, you produce luscious cherries for critters in the woods to have their fill of. You finally see your real purpose. Had you not surrendered, you would have missed it all.

THE GLORY OF GOD

As I walk with God, I am being restored, more and more each day. I'm committed to trusting God no matter what comes my way. Job said, **"Though He [*God] slay me, yet will I trust in Him . . ."** (Job 13:15; KJV; [*word added]).

That's the kind of faith I want to have. And I *can* have it because of God's character. I can trust Him with my life. He is perfect in every way, Holy, just, fair, all-loving, all-powerful, and trustworthy. He knew me before I was even born, **"For you created my inmost being; you knit me together in my mother's womb,"** (Psalm 139:13; NIV).

Furthermore, God sent His only Son to take my sins and my punishment upon Himself. I owed a debt I couldn't pay and He paid a debt He didn't owe. He offers eternal life to every living soul on the planet, but He is a gentleman. He will not force anyone to accept His gift. It's your choice and mine.

I'm so glad I rededicated my life to Jesus. Through Him I am loved, I have purpose, and I have peace. Will there be trials in this life? Yes. But God promises to never leave or forsake us. The challenges may be hard at times, but that's how our faith will increase, leading us to a closer fellowship with Him.

How glorious it must have been to be Moses, to walk up the mountain into God's very presence. God even let Moses view Him from behind, (because no human being can look into the face of God and live).

I serve a *mighty* God, the creator of the universe. And yet He calls me friend, not because I deserve it but because of His great love for me. You can know His love, too. Why wouldn't you want to? Isn't it time for you to examine your heart?

CHAPTER TWENTY-FIVE

A SONG IN MY HEART

God has blessed me in so many ways. And being part of the music program at Beulah was how He put a song in my heart once again. I sang in the choir; Steve also called upon me to sing solos now and then on a Sunday morning. And I took part in a quartet with Steve and his wife and another member. We sang four-part harmony together, taking on hymns, and songs by the Brooklyn Tabernacle, for example.

In a short time, the church moved to its new building and Steve needed a full-time music secretary. I needed a job so I jumped at the chance. It would be so much better than working in the insurance industry. The pay wasn't as good, but I could make a living, and I was happy; truly happy.

I learned a lot about music directing from Steve. I learned how to choose songs and make the service flow, how to work with a Pastor, how to keep the singers and musicians content, and how to run a rehearsal. There was so much to take in. I tucked it all away in the back of my mind, not knowing that someday I'd have a chance to apply it.

I also got back on the drums once in a while for services. The orchestra had a drummer, but he didn't mind sharing his chair.

I remember one Sunday, I was asked to accompany a ballad. I felt the use of "brushes" would be appropriate instead of sticks. Later, after the service, Steve smiled and said all that was missing were the smoke and blue lights. I guess I created a certain *mood* through the music and made it sound kind of *jazzy.*

Another time, the choir and orchestra were getting ready for a Christmas cantata. We had several rehearsals; my part was simply to sing alto in the choir.

The night of the performance, the drummer came down sick and couldn't be there. So Steve turned to me and said, "I need you to play drums tonight."

I was horrified. I said, "Steve! I haven't practiced with the band on the drums. Yes, I know the songs, but I haven't even seen the drum charts or paid attention to those parts. I can't!"

He said, "Yes you can. I've heard you practicing the drums many times on Sunday afternoons when you thought no one was here. I have complete confidence in you. Besides, we really need you."

I gulped and said, "Okay." I was really scared. I didn't know if I could pull it off, but when the time came, I sat down behind those drums and waited for the count-in. And I played through every chart without a hitch. I blew myself away! Steve was thrilled and the band and choir had a great presentation that night. Thank you, Jesus.

GOD OPENED ANOTHER DOOR

Steve was a blessing to me and I was a blessing to him. So, it's not that I wanted to leave my job, but I was thinking about going back to school, again. I had my sites set on getting a Christian education; something Bible based with an outcome in a related field.

One day, I shared my thoughts with Steve and he said, "There's only one school in this whole wide world I would recommend: Toccoa Falls College."

"Where is that," I asked.

"It's in Georgia, U.S.A."

"U.S.A.?"

"Yes. It's an amazing school and you need to go there."

Wow. I didn't expect him to tell me *that.* I had considered several colleges in Canada, but I hadn't contemplated leaving the country.

CURIOSITY AND GOD'S LEADING

Out of curiosity, I checked out this college in Toccoa. I ordered a catalog from them and looked over their majors and the costs, etc. And I prayed the Lord would show me what He wanted me to do.

I looked at several other schools in the U.S. but my mind kept drifting back to Toccoa. I believed God was saying there was something there for me, so I applied. I sent my transcripts from my previous schools and inquired about student loans.

The admissions counselor said everything looked good. I checked with the Canadian government and they said I would be eligible for a student loan. I guess I had all my ducks in a row, and my next question was, "When do I leave?"

I did have to break the news to my parents. My stepdad was okay with it but my mom was very sad. When I was a child she used to say, "Kathy, just promise me that when you're older you won't move far, far away."

I remembered her heart cry and I felt terribly guilty for going against her wishes, but I was being led by God to go. I was being called there and I couldn't, *not* do it.

My mother cried. And I'm sure she shed many tears on her pillow at night. But she understood that God was steering my boat now and she trusted in Him, too.

A COLD DAY IN JANUARY

I thought I would leave in the summer of 1992. But God had other ideas. I know His timing is perfect. So I changed my plans and decided to move in January of that year.

I couldn't take much with me. I still had my little 1977 Honda Civic, and I packed it to the *hilt.* I put the rest of my belongings into a storage locker knowing I'd have to pay rent on it every month.

I left on the morning of January 9, 1992. It was minus 25 (F) in Edmonton that day. It was so cold, my driver's door lock froze and I couldn't latch my door shut. So I grabbed a bungee cord and strung it from the right inside door handle to the left . . . and off I went.

The church staff prayed for me the day before, laying hands on my car in a mighty prayer of faith. Steve wasn't sure If the car was road worthy and he added prayers, asking God to protect me and get me all the way there.

My travels took me straight down the province of Alberta to the U.S. border. I crossed and got as far as Denver, Colorado that night. It was snowing hard.

I pulled into the first motel I saw and rented a room. In the morning, my little car was snowed in. I didn't have a shovel so I unpacked my music stand from the back and used that. Once I cleared the snow, I hopped in to start the car. But it wouldn't start. Now, what was I going to do?

Peering through my frosted eyelashes I saw a Honda dealership half a block away! Thank you, Jesus!!

I walked over to the shop and they sent someone right away to fix me up. Apparently, I needed a new battery. I purchased one and they installed it and I was on the road again.

SUNSHINE ON THE HORIZON

It took a couple more days to get to warmer weather. New Mexico was great but I couldn't wait to get to the gulf coast as fast as I could. Then I planned to drive east on Highway 10, and hopefully see a little beach and some sunshine.

Today, I tell folks that I drove straight south to El Paso, Texas, and turned left. (Kind of like Bugs Bunny, but he turned left at Albuquerque.)

I arrived in Toccoa on January 17th without any more hiccups. I was housed, temporarily for the weekend and looked forward to registration on Monday.

SETTLING IN

I didn't want to live on campus. I wasn't interested in student social life. I wanted to study and be serious. I did end up sharing an apartment with two other girls, off campus. Actually, it was a garage that had been converted into living space . . . but as you know, I've lived in worse places.

My next task besides getting my class schedule organized was to find a church. I started at Toccoa Church of God, a Pentecostal church. I loved it there, mostly because their piano player was awesome. He was so skilled.

But God spoke to my heart and told me *His* plan was better. I found another Pentecostal church called Faith Memorial. What I loved there were the people. It was a much smaller congregation and everyone was like family. So I stayed and once again God's wisdom shone through.

First of all, I met a lifelong friend there named Joanne. She was an older lady that took to me right away. Second, she played a major role in my life as a support, a prayer warrior, a teacher/adviser, and a sort of mother. I would never have made it through school if it hadn't been for her. But let me tell you about the other folks at church and my first impressions of Georgia.

A STRANGE LAND

Faith Memorial Assembly of God served as a window into a culture I had never seen before. It was a learning experience, becoming accustomed to this local way of life.

Let me assure you I'm not making fun of anyone but being from Canada and coming to live in the deep South was very interesting, to say the least.

The weather, the customs, and by all means that long, slow, southern drawl sure got my attention.

There was this one older lady at church who kept me on pins and needles; I was hardly able to control my fascination with her. When she talked to the Pastor in that old-time drawl, and I mean r-e-a-l old-timey Georgia Southern, I couldn't help snicker to myself.

I'll never forget how she used to mention her prayer requests before the congregation. It went something like this:

"Pa-ah-ster J-a-a-ick? Ey-ed lac fer y'all to re-meh-am-ber ma seester in pra-ya-er . . ."

I thought my hearing had gone bad. She could stretch a word into more syllables than was possible. It was something only an old-time, Southern lady could do. Sometimes I couldn't even understand what she was saying.

On occasion, I'd elbow the person next to me and ask, "What did she say?" But if I happened to sit next to someone who also had an accent, I was still lost in space.

When I asked, I was told, "She said, 'Pastor Jack, I'd like for y'all to remember my sister in prayer.'"

"Oh." I was amazed. Is that *really* what she said? I tried to process it all and then put it out of my mind. I thought that in time I'd get used to it. And I did learn to understand gentle old sweethearts like her as if I was raised with them. Isn't God good?

Now, several years later, hearing this drawl all the time has changed my accent a little, too. I don't sound Canadian anymore so people have stopped looking at me "funny." Of course, I don't have a drawl either, but I have picked up a very slight twang.

A TROPICAL PARADISE

I have come to love Georgia and I am thrilled to be here. Another aspect of this region is the weather.

In western Canada, the winter air around us would freeze to unbelievable depths. The voice on the radio giving the weather report each morning would mention the temperature but would emphasize how many minutes, or even seconds it would take for exposed flesh to freeze.

Usually, we had a two-minute warning. So standing at the bus stop was challenging. We had to not only dress warmly in layers but also cover our faces. I still had to go to school and folks needed to go to work. It was harsh.

Today, I see no more ice covering everything, no more snow four or five feet deep, no more nine months of winter and three months of poor skiing, (okay, that's stretching it a bit), and no more minus 30 (F) degrees below zero, making life more miserable than words can say.

All I know is, "Dang. I'm in Georgia, U.S. of A., and I'm never going back. Hallelujah! Thank You, God."

It would seem that all was well as I settled into this new world of mine. I never imagined how much trouble was lurking around the corner. But as Christians, God uses difficulties in our lives to stretch and grow our faith. I was about to get stretched.

CHAPTER TWENTY-SIX

TRYING NOT TO PANIC

I was in my first semester when I got a notice from the Canadian government that they had to "adjust" my loan. They informed me that because I chose to study *out of the country,* they could only cover *half* of my bill. What!?

All of a sudden I had a formidable problem. I thought about it and tried to think my way through it, but there was no solution in sight.

At church that following Sunday, Joanne could see that I looked troubled so she asked me what was wrong. I told her and she said, "We're going to need to do some serious praying. Come on over to my house after church and we'll have lunch and then bring this matter before the Lord."

That afternoon, we both knelt in front of her sofa and she prayed. It wasn't a begging or a pleading kind of prayer. It was a prayer of faith. We both believed God had not brought me this far to abandon me. She believed He would work it out, somehow.

Her prayers were comforting until my mind drifted back into panic mode. I did *not* want to go back to Edmonton. But I didn't know how I was going to pay my school bill. The policy of the school was "pay or leave." They did not extend credit.

A RAY OF HOPE

A week later, Joanne called me aside at church and invited me over again. At lunch, she told me she had a plan. This lady I had only known for a couple of months invited me to stay at her home, rent-free. She lived by herself and had three bedrooms so there was lots of room.

I moved out, into my 13-foot camper and stayed for the remainder of my college days plus a year after I graduated; that added up to about four years. It was difficult at times, especially in the winter when a propane tank lasted only three days. Sometimes I would run out of fuel in the middle of the night and I'd wake up cold and tired. I'd have to go outside and switch tanks so I could fire up the heater again.

Camper life was a hardship in a way, but I had the complete isolation I needed to study and rest. God was so good to me.

SAD NEWS FROM HOME

At the end of my fourth semester at school, my mother started getting ill. She had experienced a bout with cancer five years prior but now it had returned. I flew up to see her during Fall break. She was still at home, mostly staying in bed trying to fight this awful disease.

I remember laying next to her, crying. I told her how sorry I was that I disappointed her by moving far, far away.

I also apologized for all the heartache I caused her during my teens and twenties. She was so sweet. She told me how glad she was that I had come back to the Lord and how proud of me she was that I was going to a Christian school.

As for moving away, she was over it and said she forgave me long ago. She was happy for me and wanted me to do well.

The following month, in November, my mom passed away. I was supposed to write my final exams in a couple of weeks and I had five essays to turn in for various classes. I went to the Dean of the school and explained my situation.

He in turn went to all my professors and asked them to grant me an extension. They agreed, but only because up to that point I was a 4.0 student and was on the Dean's list every semester. They felt they could trust me to get the work done when I returned.

I flew home to bury my mom on November 8th. I stayed home with my stepdad until mid-January. He needed help moving out of their three-story duplex into a small apartment.

It was hard moving him in the dead of winter. We also had to take a lot of his excess belongings to an indoor flea market to sell. He was low on funds and needed cash.

I decided to empty my storage locker and sell off some of my things, too. The rest of what I wanted to keep I shipped back to Georgia via the post office. In between all of that, I was still studying for my finals and writing those five essays that were due.

JOURNEY TO INNER HEALING

I made it back home and completed all my assignments satisfactorily. So, by now I should have blossomed into a confident young woman. But I hadn't. There was still something wrong deep inside and I didn't know what it was.

Our school had a counseling department for the students. The counselor I chose to see, Mr. Harris, was also one of my professors. I spent over a year in his office, seeing him every week or two. It took that long to unload everything I had experienced and find that inner healing I needed. It wasn't a deliverance issue but rather a personality issue.

The best kind of inner healing comes from God. He knows our hearts through and through, even better than we know ourselves. He knows what we *do* need and what we *don't* need. And if we allow it, He will arrange our lives according to *His* will with our best interests in mind; He will *never* steer us wrong.

Jesus said, ***"If you continue in My word, you are truly My disciples. Then you will know the truth, and the truth will set you free,"*** (John 8:31b, 32; BSB).

THE GOAL OF COUNSELING

The whole goal of counseling is to find the truth. Why are you troubled? What could be causing it? How can you be at peace in your situation? What will bring resolve? Can you fix it? Is there room for confession? What is God saying? What are God's plans and purpose for your life?

Why was I troubled? Because I felt like I didn't fit in anywhere. I was socially awkward. If I saw someone I knew walking down the street, I'd cross over to the other side.

How was I able to be on stage then, in front of all those people? Well, that's easy. I hid behind the drums or my guitar and music stand! Between sets, I would either sit with my band, play video games, go outside, or up to my room.

What about school? What about having friends, eating lunch in the cafeteria, going to events, or speaking up in class?

I kept to myself. I only had a couple of friends. I didn't eat in the cafeteria. I didn't go to events. I rarely spoke up in class. The counselor said I had a mild case of "Avoidant Personality Disorder."

So we examined every heartache in my life. We sifted through all the hurts and disappointments. And together we learned there was good reason for me to feel and behave the way I did. But that couldn't be an excuse to continue this way. I wanted to be *whole* and the Lord wanted that for me, too.

185

THE TRUTH OF GOD'S WORD

Mr. Harris and I began to examine the truths in God's word. Passages I had read before came alive and took on new meaning. The Bible is a book that continually unfolds before us as we explore its contents, level by level. It's a book we can never outgrow.

When we hear the phrase, "God loves you," we often smile and dismiss it or say, "Yes, I know," and let it go at that.

If we meditate on what His word means, we will be affected in a much deeper way. Consider the following:

"See how very much our Father loves us, for he calls us his children, and that is what we are!" (1 John 3:1a; NLT).

"God decided in advance to adopt us into his own family by bringing us to himself through Jesus Christ. This is what he wanted to do, and it gave him great pleasure . . . to the praise of the glory of His grace, by which He made us accepted in the Beloved," (Ephesians 1:5; NLT; 1:6; NKJV).

This last verse struck a chord with me. I once again heard that I was "accepted in the beloved." God opened the door to my heart, and there in Mr. Harris' office, I heard in a much deeper way that I was accepted (and acceptable).

I pounded my fist on his desk and said, "I'm okay! I have every right to live and breathe just like anyone else. I don't have to hide, cower, or apologize for existing. God created me intentionally and His love is not only directed at the world in general; He loves me, personally. Wow . . ."

What I heard that day was God's truth. I saw in His word how He views and thinks of me.

"How precious also are Your thoughts to me, O God! How great is the sum of them! If I should count them, they would be more in number than the sand; When I awake, I am still with You," (Psalm 139:17-18; NKJV).

"For I know the thoughts that I think toward you, says the Lord, thoughts of peace and not of evil, to give you a future and a hope," (Jeremiah 29:11; NKJV).

THE GRASS LOOKED GREENER

When I walked out of Mr. Harris' office that day, the grass looked greener, the sky was brighter, and the air was fresher.

As I met people along the walkway I didn't cross over to the other side. I said hello and smiled with my head held high.

I was healed of my fears. I could stand on my own two feet without apologizing for taking up space. No one knew about my struggles because I hid them very well. But *I* knew. And every awkward moment made me want to die a thousand deaths.

I continued with my counseling sessions just a bit longer. Mr. Harris told me that in life, everyone experiences social anxiety. It's normal. But it shouldn't debilitate me. I should recognize it and then let it pass.

Moreover, because I am naturally introverted by nature, it was going to take me a little more effort to connect with people. And finally, I had missed a lifetime of building social skills. So, now I'd have to begin the process, and I shouldn't be too hard on myself.

I took all of his advice to heart and have slowly learned to interact more confidently with others. Do I still struggle? At times, I still do. But it's not the end of the world. I'm okay, God created me, and I have just as much of a right to be here as anyone else.

This time of healing broke the last stronghold off of my life. I was finally free . . . to live.

CHAPTER TWENTY-SEVEN

MY LITTLE CAR

Remember, earlier, I told you my car was famous? Well, I was still driving that 1977 Honda, but the rust on it was growing at an alarming rate, and the holes in the floorboard were getting bigger, so you could see the road.

People all over the campus knew that little car and it became rather famous. Some folks said whenever they saw me in it, they prayed. I knew its days were numbered . . . and so were my final days at Toccoa Falls College.

ONE MORE CHALLENGE

A year or so before I graduated, my sweet little Honda started feeling ill. It didn't want to go up hills anymore. That was certainly putting a limit on where I could go, including school. The campus sits in a deep valley. It was quite a struggle to travel back up that hill to go home.

I took it to a couple of mechanics but no one could figure it out. Finally, I realized it was time to retire her . . . but I didn't have any money to buy another vehicle. What was I to do?

I talked it over with friends at school and church. I did find a Nissan station wagon for about $1800 but still didn't know how I could pay for it. Then someone suggested I try to get a loan at the Bank of Toccoa. So, I went to the bank and spoke to a man I was referred to there.

I sat facing him at his desk and explained my situation. We talked about my income and my monthly expenses. It seemed I had a small amount of capital from which to make payments. But against me was the fact that I had zero collateral. He wrapped up the meeting and said he'd "let me know."

I wasn't hopeful but did hear from him in a few days. He asked me to come back to the bank so he could explain some things to me.

Here's what he said . . .

IT WAS A MATTER OF CHARACTER

"Miss Frost, I have studied your circumstances and do agree that you have enough funds to make small monthly loan payments. But my problem is that we have no way to secure this loan as you don't have any assets to use as collateral . . ."

My downcast expression was poking through my calm exterior. He continued.

". . . Miss Frost, I also see that you have a sincere need here and I've been wondering how I could help . . . so I called the school and spoke to the Dean so that I might get sort of a character check up on you.

"It turns out that you are a 4.0 student with exemplary attendance, you're a hard worker, and you present yourself with meritorious conduct . . . To me, a person's reputation is as important, if not more important, than any collateral they may possess . . . So on that basis, I will grant you this loan."

I cannot describe how relieved I was to be rescued in this way. I *was* a hard worker, and I've always believed that hard work pays. But I also have a mighty God on my side who has helped me and sent me to this compassionate man in the world of banking; this man made a difference in my life.

RECEIVING MY DEGREE AND BEYOND

My college degree reflected a double major in psychology and Christian counseling. Receiving my degree was a thrill. I wished I could have shared my success with my mother but she was gone. I was so happy that Joanne was there to see me walk across the platform and later throw my hat in the air. She was like a second mom to me.

Yes, I finished well. I almost maintained my GPA, but it dropped to 3.97 upon graduation because of a "B-" in history, and an "A-" in Western Thought and Culture. Oh well. When you go for a job, nobody asks to see your grades, anyhow.

Looking back, I believe I chose to study psychology because I wanted to discover what was wrong with *me.* Once God led me to the answers, my interest in psychology waned. Besides, I wasn't gifted with "discernment," meaning I could counsel "by the book," but I couldn't discern people's hidden motives. I was not a good fit for this kind of work.

I did try working in the field. I was employed at a crisis counseling center for over a year; I started there during my senior year. I would do the initial intake of patients; monitor their vital signs, and observe them during my shift. I also wrote reports to the doctors, ran group therapy, and supervised their entertainment periods.

I got a good taste of being a support counselor, but truthfully, it wasn't my cup of tea. When school was over, I kept my hours there to weekend-only, twelve-hour shifts. During the weekdays I continued full-time at the ministry, and in the evenings I continued to work in the computer lab at school, helping students.

Why so many jobs? Well, I had a student loan and a car loan to pay, although my school bill wasn't that high compared to other students. That's because I worked my way through college and God did bless me with a financial gift in my second year.

WEDDING BELLS

My stepdad had been single for almost two years. But he was very lonely after my mother died. Then I heard he was moving to Victoria, B.C. When I asked him about it he said he was getting married.

The wedding was set for late May of 1996. I had graduated earlier that month so I was free to travel there with the time off work, and take part in his wedding.

They were married on a boat, out in the ocean. It was all very romantic and sweet. I wished them the best as I departed.

After the wedding, my stepdad and his new wife continued living at her home in Victoria. Her teenage son also lived there. Unfortunately, he was becoming a problem. He was messy and noisy and disrespectful. My dad had many run-ins with him. That drove a wedge into my dad's marriage and after a couple of years, they divorced.

Dad moved to Kelowna and settled into a small, efficiency apartment. He decided to give up his car and get a city bus pass instead. He enjoyed meandering all over town, meeting people, and volunteering at senior care facilities. And so, that's how his life went for the next several years.

THINKING ABOUT "LOVE"

When I was living in the world without Jesus at the helm, I always had a boyfriend. Typically, it is said about relationships that men are looking for sex and women are looking for love.

Without trying to lay blame I'd have to say that if either of my dad's loved me, they were dysfunctional about showing it. My real dad was a perfectionist and I felt I could never please him no matter what I did or didn't do.

My stepdad could be rather distant and he didn't offer much physical affection. And if my behavior should slip out of line, he would communicate that by ignoring me. Sometimes he wouldn't speak a word to me for two or three weeks. I'd have to ask my mother what I did and she could usually tell me.

Additionally, both dads had explosive tempers. And their outbursts were very hard on me and my mother. We shed many private tears.

Having a boyfriend fulfilled my need to be held, supported, and loved. I could reveal my innermost secrets and be heard. That was important because I wasn't a social creature and never had many friends.

The problem was, my choices in men were awful. They had dysfunctions of their own and eventually, I would leave them or they would leave me.

Now, here I was, a college graduate with no real plans for the future, and no boyfriend or prospects for marriage. I had not dated in approximately ten years since I turned my life over to God in 1987.

LOOKING IN ALL THE WRONG PLACES

I prayed every day that the Lord would bring someone special into my life. But this time it had to be someone *He* chose. I clearly wasn't capable of choosing the right person.

So I waited and prayed and waited some more. This is kind of funny, but while I was still in school, in my final year, there was a man in my class studying to be a Pastor. I was attracted to him and was wishing he would notice me.

When I saw him from afar, walking along, I would sit down at one of the benches along the way, primp up my hair, and straighten my clothes. Then I'd smile at him as he walked by. But he didn't even know I existed. *Sheesh.*

I'm here to tell you, God doesn't need any help. He is perfectly able to pick the right person at the right time.

GOD'S TAPESTRY

One of my co-workers at the ministry office, Linda, invited me to her house for supper one night. What I didn't know was that she had also invited a man over that used to host Bible studies there quite often.

His name was Doug. He was an older man, but quite handsome with blonde hair and blue eyes. After supper, Linda's husband, Mike invited me to jam with him. He was a drummer, extraordinaire; he played in the style of Buddy Rich.

I still remembered some of the jazz numbers I used to sing. I had my guitar with me and played a few of my old songs while Mike played along with me. It was fun, and everyone was quite impressed.

I also brought my scrapbook over to share some of my history with Linda and her family. One of the pictures was of a quartet I sang in with Steve, the music director at Beulah. Doug was looking over my shoulder when he blurted out, "Hey. I know that guy." He was referring to Steve.

I said, "No you don't"

"Yes, I do," he insisted. "His name is Steve Reibsome.

"Well, his name is printed right there!" (I rolled my eyes.)

I didn't know if that was a "come-on" line or what. As for the tapestry God was weaving, it turns out Doug and Steve *had* met years ago. Doug had invited Steve and two other students to share his house on campus. They were planning to move in the weekend of November 5, but somehow, their plans were delayed.

In the early morning of November 6, the water dam above the college gave way and a wall of water roared through the campus at a height of 55 feet high, traveling 110 miles per hour. The disaster destroyed everything. Steve's plans never did materialize, but Doug and Steve remained somewhat connected for the next twenty years. Imagine that. How strange that I worked with this same man, years later.

I WAS A "KNIGHTESS" IN SHINING ARMOR

I thought Doug was nice, but I didn't think much more about him after that evening. That was July of 1996.

Then, in November, a call came into the office one day and my co-worker answered it.

"Hello. _____ Ministries," she said

"Hi, Linda? Is that you?"

"Yes, hi Doug. It's me. What's up?"

"Well, I'm up here near Nashville, Tennessee, and my car broke down. They checked it out and they said I threw a rod in the engine. I'm going to leave the car here, but I need to find someone who could pick me up and bring me home . . ."

I was standing next to Linda trying to listen. Linda paused and turned to me explaining what he just said. We both stood in silence for a moment.

"Hello, Linda? are you there?"

"Yes, yes, Doug, I'm here . . ."

The wheels in my head started turning. I didn't remember this man by name, so I whispered to Linda, "Who is this guy? Is he a decent person? Would I be safe going to get him?

"Yes, oh yes. You know him. You met him at my house a couple of months ago; he came for dinner."

"Oh . . . okay, yes. I remember . . . well . . . tell him I'll come to get him after work."

So, like a "knightess" in shining armor, I finished work early and left for Monteagle, Tennessee at three o'clock, grabbing a burger along the way. It took me five hours to get to his motel. He was waiting outside and greeted me warmly. Then, we went to Shoney's restaurant for refreshments before heading home.

Doug was a very good conversationalist and we spoke easily with each other about everything under the sun. He was a strong Christian believer and so was I so we had a good foundation from which to communicate.

And guess what? Doug and his crew built the ministry building I worked out of. I praised him for the amazing job he did. I thought he was very skilled and talented.

We got back to Toccoa at about two in the morning. He bid me farewell and thanked me profusely. He said he would stop by my workplace the next day. I wasn't sure why, but I didn't mind the idea at all.

CHAPTER TWENTY-EIGHT

THE RED STREAK

I went to work the next day feeling a bit weary but I was intrigued by the fact that I couldn't get Doug out of my mind. As the day wore on I started feeling disappointed, though, thinking he wasn't going to stop by after all.

Then about three o'clock in the afternoon, I saw this red streak go by my office window. What was *that?* I looked outside to see Doug getting out of a little red Toyota, Celica. I gasped. Did my hair look okay? Had my makeup worn off in spots? Good grief.

He came in the back door and came right to my office. On my desk, he set down a steaming cup of coffee in a pretty glass mug. His arms were full of gifts but he managed to give me a hug and then gave me a teddy bear, some chocolate donuts, a blue heart-shaped vase with flowers, and a card. (I guess he was covering all the bases.)

We said our hellos and he proceeded to thank me again for coming to get him the night before. Our eyes glistened at each other. I knew something was stirring; romance was in the air.

He asked me if I was free for supper and I said yes. From that day forward we saw each other every day.

NOTHING BUT THE FACTS, SIR

We usually met for supper when I finished work. I had an hour or so before I had to be at the computer lab. (I was still working three jobs.)

We usually met in a restaurant somewhere, but he had me over to his apartmrnt sometimes, too. He was a good cook and would prepare meals for us.

It seemed we had so much to talk about. We enjoyed each other's company and looked forward to being together. Because we were older, our courtship moved along quickly compared to young folks that commonly date a year or more.

One night in December when the computer lab was closed, we decided to go to Shoney's in the next town. I always liked their salad bar.

When we were done eating and finishing our tea, Doug sort of got serious. He leaned forward and said, "Kathy, we've been seeing each other every day now but the truth is, I don't know that much about you. I don't even know how old you are."

Loaded with facts, I leaned forward and said, "Doug Veer, you were born in 1937 and you're 59 years old. I was born in 1959 and I'm 37 years old. Do you have a *problem* with that?"

He was stunned. "Oh . . ." he said. "Well, I was just asking because I think I'm falling in love with you." Then *I* was stunned. I said, "I think I love you, too."

As I departed to go home that night he leaned inside my car window and gave me his first kiss. I had peace in my heart and believed God was drawing us together.

WHOOPS!

A couple of weeks later, we were wrapping Christmas gifts at his house. We were just talking about this and that when out of the blue he said, "Kathy, will you marry me?"

That was followed by, "Whoops, oh, my goodness! That just slipped right out. I didn't mean to say that, but . . . I did. I should have been more formal about it. So let me get down on my knees and say Kathy, would you do me the honor of being my wife?"

I was floored. I didn't know what to say, but it was music to my ears. I said, "Yes!" That weekend we picked a tentative wedding date. Then we went shopping for rings. We picked out a beautiful setting; the engagement ring had a large, heart-shaped diamond. The wedding band fit into it perfectly.

A WORRISOME CONFESSION

Another month went by when Doug took me aside for another serious conversation. I guess he felt he had made another *whoops.*

"Kathy, I hope I have not been too hasty, but we haven't been dating that long--about eight weeks now--and maybe it was too soon to ask you for your hand in marriage. Please don't be disappointed, but could we postpone it for just a little while?"

He had already shared some of his past with me. His first wife cheated on him, and then she passed away. His second wife cheated on him and they were divorced. Then she passed away.

His third wife cheated on him and caused him to go to prison because he kidnaped their two children for their own safety. Later on, they were divorced.

Since then, Doug remained single and had not dated for ten years. He said he was sold out to God and belonged to Him, alone.

I appreciated that and understood he had been "bitten" three times. *Why* would he want to do it again?

My eyes welled up with tears and I said, "Doug Veer . . . I hear where you're coming from. Yes, I'm disappointed you want to cancel it . . ."

He said, "No, no, no. Not cancel, just postpone . . . for a little while."

"Okay, well, postpone, cancel; what's the difference? But I understand. Please, take all the time you need. I'll wait for you, however long it takes."

A WEDDING IN THE AIR

Doug didn't take long to make up his mind. Two weeks went by and then we set a new date. We were married on March 8, 1997, after three and a half months of courtship.

My father and sister from Montreal had planned to come when the first date was set. But when we set the second date, it didn't leave enough time for them to arrange their travel. We all understood and it was okay. Doug and I traveled to meet my dad a year or so later and we all enjoyed getting together then.

It was a sweet little wedding with 20 or so guests. My friend, Joanne stepped in to help me. Her daughter gave me her white prom dress for the ceremony, and Joanne donated my bouquet.

We gave all the guests instant cameras and they took beautiful photos for our wedding album. I think the total cost of our wedding was $300. But we had the nicest wedding anyone could want.

After the church ceremony, we had a brief reception at Joanne's. She made the cake and provided some finger foods. Later, we had lunch at a local Chinese restaurant with Doug's daughters from out of town. And then we were off to Monteagle for our honeymoon and on to Nashville the next day.

I loved visiting Nashville and taking in all the sights. Then we went on to Martin, Tennessee to visit Doug's sister and her children and their families. We spent a little over a week away and then returned to our small apartment in Toccoa.

GOD SPOKE THROUGH A DREAM

We were quite tired the day after arriving home and decided to take an afternoon nap so without getting undressed, we laid down on the bed and fell asleep; my head rested on Doug's arm.

I don't know how much time passed; maybe 15 or 20 minutes when we woke up. I said to Doug,

"Wow. I just had the most amazing dream."

"Yes, me too! What was your dream?"

I said, "I dreamt we were working in an operating room and we were surgeons . . . and I would cut the patient open with . . ."

Doug interrupted, "With musical notes. Yes, I saw that too! And then while the patient was open . . ."

I interrupted Doug, "You placed the letters of the alphabet inside of them."

And Doug said ..... "Then you sewed them back up with . . ."

I blurted out, "With musical notes!"

We stopped talking and thought about the impossibility of two people dreaming the same dream at the same time.

Doug said, "I think I have an interpretation for our dream. I think this dream has come from the Lord and I think He is showing us our future life together. You will minister to people through music and song, and then I will preach God's word to them, and you will close out the meeting using music once again."

We were stunned and encouraged all at the same time. God was with us and He was showing us His purpose for us as a couple and how He planned to use us in ministry. We are amazed by the dream to this day and it has absolutely proven true.

MARRIED LIFE

So finally, at the age of 37, I was married. All of my past mistakes were behind me and my husband and I both gave the reins of our lives to God.

The Bible talks about relationships in various places. Here's an interesting passage from the Old Testament:

"Two are better than one because they have a good reward for their efforts. For if either falls, his companion can lift him up; but pity the one who falls without another to lift him up. Also, if two lie down together, they can keep warm; but how can one person alone keep warm? And if someone overpowers one person, two can resist him. A cord of three strands is not easily broken," (Ecclesiastes 4:9-12; CSB.)

Two people, together, can lean on each other for support. But when the two intertwine themselves with God, it is a three-strand-winning team. The three strands in our marriage were Doug, myself, and God. Because of that, we have been so blessed.

When we got married we agreed we would never speak the word, *divorce.* We were committed, "until death do us part."

So divorce, never, but murder? (Lol.) There were days when we might have wanted to arrange that . . . *just kidding!* I don't mean that literally. There *are* ups and downs in every marriage but being determined to work through the issues creates something valuable to be thankful for.

Doug and I have some differences. He is 22 years older than me, he's American, I'm Canadian, He grew up with 13 brothers and sisters, I grew up an only child, he's a multi-tasker and a nurturer, I a single-focused and I'm not a nurturer, he's more the dependent type and very outgoing, and I'm independent and introverted.

At the same time, our skill sets complement each other. He cooks, I clean, (although we're both tidy), he preaches, I sing, he does the yard work, and I do the household budget. And of course, we have other things in common, too.

GOING FORWARD IN MINISTRY

Over the years, God has used us in His kingdom work. We have been involved in prison ministry for a couple of decades. Inmates need hope. We bring Jesus Christ to them and if they're serious about their walk with God, the Lord does change them from the inside out. We've seen the results and it's a beautiful thing.

We have done a lot of work at Augusta State Medical Prison. We would go in once a month to bring services and pray with the men. For a couple of years, we went in once a week so I could organize and set up a band and choir.

I provided all the printed music. It was a collection of lead sheets in binders. Also, I helped one man learn the bass guitar. I don't play bass but I knew enough about it to put the right materials into his hands. He embraced it all and grew by leaps and bounds.

I gave pointers to various drummers from time to time and guided the group with ensemble playing. I also taught a class there once in music theory so they could be a bit more educated about how to read music.

Let me tell you more about prison ministry . . .

CHAPTER TWENTY-NINE

THE PRISON WARDEN

Wardens do transfer to different facilities from time to time. And each one has his own philosophy of how things should be run. When we first started volunteering at Augusta State, the warden at the time was a Christian. We met with him on a few occasions, mostly to ask for special favors.

The security protocol for prisons is quite strict. If you're caught bringing in a cell phone you *will* go to jail. But there are a lot of other things you can't bring in, either. Everything must be examined at the door.

You *must* pass through a metal detector and all bags *must* be transparent plastic or they will also be thoroughly inspected. Either way, they go through a scanner just like at the airport. No stone is left unturned. So, asking for and receiving a special request is almost impossible.

WHEN GOD IS IN IT

This particular warden had a heart for inmates. So, when we asked if we could bring in pizzas and coke to celebrate the work the band was doing, he allowed it. Normally, that would be considered *contraband,* but he gave us permission.

Once we shared our plans with the men they looked forward to it, and when it happened they were thrilled.

A few months later, we approached the warden again. This time we wanted to use the gymnasium to bring an Easter program into the prison and invite the entire prison population. We had just performed a play at church portraying the crucifixion of Jesus. Now, we wanted to present it to the inmates.

The program included around 15 fully costumed actors, a cross, and fake blood. Most wardens would have given us an absolute, "No." But this Warden, recognized full well that the Gospel is powerful. He also knew Doug and me. And being prison ministers, we had proven our trustworthiness to keep security protocols intact, so, he said, "Yes. Go ahead and bring them in."

The prison houses 1200 inmates and of course, we would have loved to minister to all of them but I think we had about 200 inmates come out on that special day.

Surely, when God is in it, He will win it. We have been grateful to Him over the years for allowing us to minister in the prisons and see lives changed.

GOING FORWARD IN MUSIC

Doug's calling is evangelism. We have traveled to many towns in Georgia and out of state to minister in churches as well as other jails and prisons. I would always bring special music with a song or two. We have ministered to many folks and have seen many people give their lives to Jesus.

In the year 2000, I felt the Lord calling me to record a CD project. I chose mostly cover tunes but I did include two originals. I had the background tracks to my songs recorded at Christian World Music out of Oklahoma. I sent them the sheet music, and they used their session players to create my tracks.

I recorded all of my lead vocals and some background vocals myself. I did some songs in the spare room at Joanne's house. I did the rest of them in the upstairs closet of our tiny apartment. I used a Joe Meek condenser microphone and it was so powerful that when our next-door neighbors would come home I could hear them in my headphones as they came in their door, downstairs.

One more tidbit about the recording project. The first song track was created from scratch. I played guitar, I created the bass track from a CD containing bass snippets, I used the same CD to create piano fills and banjo fills, I programmed the drum machine, and I laid down the background vocals. It was a blast to create the entire band myself.

Because I was so fussy about the final product, my CD didn't get finished for 11 more years. The project was dormant for a long time because I got discouraged, but my friends and family kept asking when it would be done and I know the Lord wanted me to press on with it. I finally finished it and put it on Amazon.

I'm so blessed that God helped and encouraged me otherwise I would have walked away from it forever. But it was His will that I return to it so I did and through it, I blessed others and honored Him.

GOD WEAVES HIS TAPESTRY

I have to say, Doug and I have so many connections with each other that only the Lord could have designed such a cohesive blueprint. This husband He brought into my life was connected to me through some of the same people we both knew from years ago.

Doug knew Steve, as mentioned earlier. Doug also knew "of" my Pastor, Albert Runge, at Beulah. Pastor Runge went to Nyack Bible College in New York, and Doug's adopted dad, Rev. Harold Ronson also went to Nyack. He and Runge were roommates and sang in a quartet. Dad Ronson was a mentor in Doug's life just as Joanne had been in mine.

Speaking of Joanne, Doug knew her too. When Joanne first moved to Toccoa in the 80s as a single mom with her four children, she needed a place to live until she could arrange a place to settle. Doug met her through work associates and invited her and her kids to stay with him.

Now, years later, she in turn invited me to live with her when I had nowhere else to go. Without her prayers and her helping hand, I surely would have had to turn back. But God used her in a mighty way.

As my relationship with Doug was approaching marriage, I said to Joanne one day,

"Joanne, I must confess that I've been dating an older Christian man and we are now talking about getting married. I don't know if you've ever met him in your travels, but would you know Doug Veer?"

Joanne said, "Doug Veer! Why yes, I know him well." And she proceeded to tell me about how she and her children stayed at his house for a spell.

God works in mysterious ways. Here we were from two different countries, with 22 years difference in our ages, and yet the puzzle pieces of our lives fit together so perfectly. Only God could paint such a profoundly intricate picture. It makes me cry out,

"Oh, God. I just want to fall down and worship at your feet. You are such a great and mighty God. Thank you for making my life so full and beautiful."

TRUSTING GOD IN ALL THINGS

In 2006, I was diagnosed with Rheumatoid Arthritis. I've done everything I could to naturally fight the disease. I did not want the heavy chemo drugs suggested because I didn't want the severe side effects including a suppressed immune system. But the trade-off was deformity.

In 2011, I was hired as music director at Gibson First Baptist Church. I led congregational praise and worship every Sunday morning and evening. During morning services I led the choir. In the evenings, I simply led worship with my guitar.

I was responsible for choosing all the musical selections, rehearsing the choir with the piano player or with tracks, and creating and rehearsing the special Easter and Christmas cantata presentations that included drama segments. And I created and organized set props and decorations for each play.

In the Spring of 2016, I found playing my guitar was becoming impossible, so after five years of ministry there, I had to resign.

Despite this disappointment, I have trusted God completely and I am content in whatever He brings my way whether I'm young or old, well or not well, rich or poor. In all these things I have His peace; the peace that passes all understanding.

My life is like a breath of air or a fading flower. It will have come and gone in a nanosecond. I know this earth is not my home. I know I will live in God's glory one day, not because I am worthy but because He is merciful. That is my focus.

PUTTING IT ALL AWAY
I think back to the days when I made guitars with rubber bands stretched over shoe boxes and twanged and strummed them as if I had something.

I fanned cardboard in front of my face as I sang so I could hear and feel the natural reverb it created.

I played with wooden spoons on empty pots and pans turned upside down, pretending they were drums. Though it may have been just noise to anyone else, it was music to me.

Sadly, time passes on. With no respect for one's age, it takes a toll on everyone. Far too soon, the horrible disease of arthritis took its toll on my joints.

When my wrists would no longer work without pain and my fingers and elbows ached from trying to play the rhythms they once loved, the tears came and I knew it was time to put it all away.

SAYING GOODBYE TO OLD FRIENDS

Today, the eyes of my guitars stare at me in their pitiful loneliness, wondering why I never come to them anymore. They don't understand that it's the pain of this poor body that has laid them aside, not the desires of my heart.

My three guitars sit silent, like faithful little soldiers waiting for their instructions which I can no longer give them. Now they just lean against their guitar stands, in my music room/office, a beautiful but gloomy reminder of the many hours I spent caressing them and listening to them as they spoke that special language that only true music lovers can hear.

And my drums and cymbals are gone, too. I've mourned over the day a man and his son came to look at my drums. I wanted to sell them but when the perspective buyers arrived I kind of hoped they wouldn't take them.

I stood quietly, watching them express their excitement and joy as they decided to agree to the purchase.

I packed my drums into their gig bags for the very last time. Now someone else would make them live again. It hurt my heart to part with them; my instruments have been the most wonderful friends I've ever known.

Even though I've lost that joy of playing instruments, God has preserved my voice. He put a song in my heart and I'll never stop sharing it. I often sing in church and sometimes lead praise and worship with background tracks. I also offer concerts in churches and prisons.

Music was planted in me *by* God and *for* God, and as long as I can, I will always use it to sing praise to Him while encouraging the world around me. Yes, I'm glad the Lord is still using me.

MY LIFE AS MRS. VEER

Neither tongue nor pen can ever clearly tell how blessed my husband and I have been. We've spent a lifetime serving God, ministering to people, and helping them. We've had opportunities to express the gifts God has placed within us, like music and writing and teaching and counseling.

We've had all of our needs met, not because we've had great riches but because of God's thoughtful provision. We've not had a lot of money but we've not had unpaid bills or gone without heat or food.

Though we've never had children together we've enjoyed sharing in the lives of Doug's grown children and families. They've struggled at times but have done well in the long run and we are so proud of them.

And after 26 years of marriage, we can declare that we've been faithful to one another and have a loving relationship to this day.

God is so good. How is it that people stubbornly want to live, serving themselves when a life with God is so much richer in every way? Looking back, we are grateful for all of His blessings and our goal is to know Him more and more each day.

CHAPTER THIRTY

CONNECTING BACK TO FAMILY ROOTS

I don't go to Montreal as often as I'd like. I used to visit almost every year until the COVID outbreak. I think it was five years between visits home.

Doug and I have maintained our family connections by phone. We'd usually speak to my dad every week or two and we would pass a lot of emails back and forth about politics, health tips, funny-looking animals, and pretty nature scenes.

My dad has always been a "bigger than life" figure for me and my sister. He was a great achiever and he accomplished much in his lifetime despite his very meager beginnings.

In the summer of 2022, his health began to decline rapidly. He discovered he had fourth-stage cirrhosis of the liver as well as kidney failure.

My sister was very close to him in part because she had run his factory for over 30 years. Around the start of July, she decided to stay at his house each night because he was getting so ill. At that point, he had begun using a walker but still had a hard time getting around. He soon digressed to a wheelchair and after falling out of bed a couple of times in the night he was transferred to the hospital.

I was supposed to travel to Montreal to see him around mid-July, but the border restrictions were impossible. There was a provision for compassionate entry into Canada without having to quarantine but I would have to get a doctor to sign a certain form.

To my shock and amazement, my dad's doctor wouldn't sign it. He said dad wasn't at the end of his life *yet.*

The problem was, I needed to submit this form four weeks before my travel date. By that time, he could have passed away.

TRYING TO FIND A WAY

Another option was to cross over and agree to quarantine for two weeks. I thought about it and decided this option was better than nothing. So I changed my flight and was all ready to go, but my COVID test the day before came back positive!

I quarantined at home for five days, (although I had no symptoms). I changed my flight yet again, and this time went for a PCR COVID test with same-day results. Thank heaven it was negative.

The nurse at the testing site explained that because I had COVID the previous year, the virus was still in my body. The rapid test I had is a crude test that automatically picks up these old virus particles, but the PCR molecular test is more sophisticated and can differentiate between old cells and active cells.

So I was good to go and arrived in Montreal on August 14th. I immediately began my quarantine until the 14 days were up. My additional tests during that time were both negative.

COPING WITH DISAPPOINTMENT

The result of liver and kidney failure is a build-up of toxins and fluids in the body, some of which cross the blood-brain barrier causing brain fog. So when I went to see my dad the first time, I'm not sure he knew I was there. He slept a lot but was awake some to drink a bit of water or eat a little chicken soup that my sister made especially for him.

He could hardly talk. Sometimes no sound came out; other times he spoke only in a whisper. When he did speak he was hard to understand.

In the days that followed we would get calls from the nurse saying he was wide awake and communicating. So we would rush over to see him but when we got there he'd be asleep again.

At one point he did wake up and I was able to tell him I was there: his long-lost daughter from Georgia. I think this time he understood. There was a flash of recognition on his face.

I then proceeded to share Jesus with him. I told him when it was his time to go, all he needed to do is call on the name of Jesus for the Bible says, ***"Anyone who calls upon the name of the Lord will be saved,"*** (Romans 10:13; TLB).

I wasn't sure if he took it in, but my sister thought he did. I also learned that he had spoken to his friend earlier, asking Jesus to take him to heaven and he envisioned Jesus coming down from the cross to walk with him.

While I didn't have one hundred percent assurance that my dad was saved, I was encouraged and at peace over this testimony.

THE HUMILITY OF NEEDING FORGIVENESS

The following week my dad took a turn for the better. My sister said it was like a miracle. He was completely lucid and recognized me as soon as I walked into the room. He called me by name and I went over and stood by his bed.

After some small talk, he wanted me to lean in so he could ask me a very serious question. He said, "Kathy, do you hold anything against me in your heart because my relationship with you was hurt when I left your mother?"

I said, "No daddy. I don't have anything against you. If there was any forgiving to be done, I forgave you many years ago. No, Daddy. Everything is okay between us."

That was such a precious moment. He had asked me this question before, years ago. But my answer was the same then, too.

I was encouraged to see his humility at this time. He did not show that side of himself as a rule. Now, maybe he could express this same humility before the Lord. I was hopeful for him.

My sister and I invited the hospital Chaplain to come to pray with my dad. We spent several moments in God's presence, thanking Him for the gift of salvation through Christ for the forgiveness of our sins. The following day, my dad passed away. It was September 17, 2022. He was 89 years old.

MY FINAL CHAPTER

As I write this final chapter, my mind drifts back to my ordeal as a two-year-old. I was deathly sick because of ruptured tonsils while my parents were trying to save my life.

Now, having just experienced my dad's terminal illness and death, it's been *his* life I've wanted to help save. But while I couldn't save him in a physical sense, I did help lead him to salvation in a spiritual sense.

Witnessing to him wasn't just a bedside conversation. I had been sharing Jesus Christ with him for 35 years, verbally and through the many letters I wrote. And family and friends had been lifting him up in prayer for at least that many years or more.

I'm confident I will see him in heaven one day. My mother and stepdad will be there, too, and many other dear loved ones as well.

In the meantime, I will continue to live out my days with my husband as we preach and sing, and glorify God. We want to see as many people saved as possible. You see, it's a matter of life and death.

IT'S NOT ABOUT RELIGION

Every human being has eternal life. But there are two destinations. People who have accepted the gift of God's Son, have asked to be forgiven of their sins, and have invited Him into their hearts to dwell, will spend eternity in heaven with God.

People who have rejected God's Son, or have relied only on their own philosophies and good works to get through the pearly gates, will spend eternity in hell. Remember, God doesn't send people there. We each have a choice.

Jesus said, ***"Not all who sound religious are really godly people. They may refer to me as 'Lord,' but still won't get to heaven. For the decisive question is whether they obey my Father in heaven. At the Judgment many will tell me, 'Lord, Lord, we told others about you and used your name to cast out demons and to do many other great miracles.' But I will reply, 'You have never been mine. Go away, for your deeds are evil,'"*** (Matthew 7:21-23; TLB).

Verse 23 in the King James version says it this way: ***"And then will I profess unto them, I never knew you: depart from me, ye that work iniquity."***

Here, the word "knew" means an intimate kind of knowing, not a superficial kind.

How can this be, you ask? The answer is simple. God sees our hearts. He knows if we name the name of God because we need a fire escape, or because we want to *know Him.* He can tell the difference between those who only seek His hand and those who seek His face.

Pause, and think of that. Imagine if you married someone and later he/she drifted off on their own, to live by themselves. Your relationship with your spouse would be broken. Yes, you could telephone now and then, but your intimacy would be gone.

Then suppose your spouse approached you one day, in need of $100,000 to cover a medical bill. You might say, "I'm not going to pay your bills for you. Get away from me. We have no connection anymore."

God feels the same way. He will not extend His kind hand to you if you have just wanted to use Him, all along.

If you want to accept the Lord into your life you can't just know *about* Him; you must *know Him*. He desires a *personal relationship* with you. He's not interested in "Sunday visitation." He wants "full-time custody." He wants to adopt you because He loves you. He doesn't want your lip service. He wants your love.

PARTING THOUGHTS

In closing, I'd like to share a devotional from Charles Stanley's book called, *Pathways to His Presence*.

(Devotional from March 21)
"In his book, The Problem of Pain, C.S.Lewis writes, 'One dynamic benefit of pain is that it shatters the illusion that we have, whether good or bad . . . Without pain, humans revert to an innate sense of self-sufficiency. We find God an interruption . . . or as a friend of mine said, We regard God as an airman regards his parachute; it's there for emergencies but he hopes he will never have to use it.'

"God is not a parachute. People do not have a ripcord with which they can pop God out of a neatly

packed backpack to help with a temporary crisis, only to be refolded and stuffed away. Without a personal, active, growing relationship with God, no one's life is complete. Sometimes, even though it hurts, it takes a dose of pain to help us remember that."

I hope this book has encouraged you as I've tried to write about the pain of my lowest lows so you could see how the power of God has lifted me up to the higher places in Him and how He has put a song in my heart, once again.

I hope also, that you have been inspired to want to seek Jesus as *your* Lord and Savior. Receiving Him is something you will never regret. I've never regretted it and I've never turned back once I fully understood what God was offering.

Would you turn to Jesus Christ and discover His love for you, today?

Psalm 40:1-3; NLT
I waited patiently for the Lord to help me,
and he turned to me and heard my cry.
He lifted me out of the pit of despair,
out of the mud and the mire.
He set my feet on solid ground
and steadied me as I walked along.
He has given me a new song to sing,
a hymn of praise to our God.
Many will see what he has done and be amazed.
They will put their trust in the Lord.

A Song In My Heart

EPILOGUE

A NOTE FROM MY HUSBAND

It has given me great joy and has been nothing short of an honor to be a part of sharing this story; a story of a life so interesting, so exciting, and yet so delicate as to move me to gratefully open my heart and be touched by this one surrendered life: the life of Kathy Veer.

Kathy's had a love for music all of her life but the hands that used to guide the drumsticks across the tightened fabric of a drumhead can no longer dance a musical rhythm into the air. And sadly, the fingers that used to delicately stretch across the slender neck of a guitar can no longer caress those strings and talk to us with the musical language they formerly spoke.

Although an enemy called arthritis has captured and now controls the once precise movement of those parts of her body, the wonderful gift God placed in her from birth still remains. It is still enjoyed by others as beautiful notes skip across her lips as she serves the Lord with her singing.

Volumes more could be said as I've tried to share Kathy's love of God and music. But I believe through these words she has opened up her soul so you could see that special place God has planted a song in her heart.

What more can be said, other than how very grateful I am to know Kathy as my God-loving, dedicated wife, and friend, who has shared her life with me . . . and here in these pages with you.

Sincerely, in Christ Jesus, R Douglas Veer

HOW TO BECOME A CHRISTIAN
❧ ❧ ❧

GOD HAS ALWAYS WANTED A PERSONAL RELATIONSHIP WITH YOU...
Even before He created you, He chose to show
His love toward you, through His
sacrifice on the cross, and through His Word.
Here are some very simple steps for understanding
salvation and becoming a Christian believer.

ADMIT TO GOD THAT YOU HAVE SINNED
The fact is, everyone sins. We need to understand this
before we can go any further.

Roman 3:23
"For all have sinned and come short
of the glory of God"

Romans 3:10-12
"As it is written: `There is no one righteous, not even one;
there is no one who understands, no one who seeks God. All
have turned away, they have together become worthless;
there is no one who does good,
not even one.'"

Unfortunately, there are consequences for our sins. It is
death. We all face physical death but anyone who is not a
Christian believer when he/she dies, will die spiritually as
well as physically and be
eternally separated from God.

Romans 6:23a
"The wages of sin is death . . . "

It's also important to know that we cannot earn salvation
based on our own merits.
We cannot be good enough, or smart enough,
or kind enough, or religious enough.

We are not only sinners, but we fall short
of the standard God requires.
SO, WHAT SHOULD WE DO?

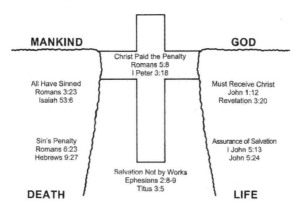

MANKIND   GOD

Christ Paid the Penalty
Romans 5:8
I Peter 3:18

All Have Sinned
Romans 3:23
Isaiah 53:6

Must Receive Christ
John 1:12
Revelation 3:20

Sin's Penalty
Romans 6:23
Hebrews 9:27

Assurance of Salvation
I John 5:13
John 5:24

Salvation Not by Works
Ephesians 2:8-9
Titus 3:5

DEATH   LIFE

BELIEVE THAT JESUS PAID FOR YOUR
SINS ON THE CROSS
When Jesus died on the cross and rose again, He paid the
full penalty for your sins and mine, and the sins of every
person, living, dead, and even yet unborn.
The only condition for receiving His salvation is that we
believe He did this for us, according to His Word.
Yes, He did it because He loves us,
and because we couldn't pay for our sins, ourselves.

John 3:16 King James Version (KJV)
"For God so loved the world, that he gave his only begotten
Son, that whosoever believeth in him should not perish, but
have everlasting life."

Romans 5:8
"God demonstrated His love toward us in that while we were
still sinners, Christ died for us."
God's word leads us to believe in Jesus Christ
as God's Son and accept Jesus' gift of forgiveness for our
sins. Along with God's forgiveness,
we will receive God's gift of eternal life.

Romans 6:23b
" . . . the gift of God is Eternal Life through
Jesus Christ our Lord"

Would you like to receive Jesus Christ into your heart and
become a Christian believer today?

Maybe you need some help; a starting point, perhaps?
Here's an example of how a person could
pray to receive salvation:

THE SINNER'S PRAYER
*"Dear God, I know that I have sinned
against you and am deserving of punishment.
But because you love me so much,
you sent your only Son, Jesus Christ,
to take the punishment that I deserve.
With your help, I place my faith and trust in You as
my Savior and Lord. Please forgive me and come into
my heart. With your help, I will live for you from this
day forward. Thank You for saving me, and for
offering me Your wonderful grace. Thank You also for
the gift of eternal life! In Jesus' name I pray, Amen!"*

In themselves, these words will not save you.
But praying in faith
and believing on Jesus Christ, will!

Romans 10:13
"Whosoever will call on the name of the Lord
shall be saved."

Romans 5:1
"Therefore, since we have been Justified through Faith,
we have Peace with God through our Lord Jesus Christ."

Romans 8:1
"Therefore, there is now no condemnation
for those who are in Christ Jesus."

John 1:12
"And as many as received Him,
and believed in His name,
to them He gave the power
to become children of God."

Romans 8:38-39
"For I am convinced that neither death nor life,
neither angels nor demons neither the present nor the
future, nor any powers, neither height nor depth,
nor anything else in all creation,
will be able to separate us from the love of God
that is in Christ Jesus our Lord."

Romans 10:9-10
"If you confess with your mouth that Jesus is Lord,
and believe in your heart that
God raised Jesus from the dead,
you shall be saved;
for with the heart man believes unto righteousness,
and with the mouth confession is made unto salvation."

WHAT'S NEXT?
Confess your faith in Jesus Christ
Share your experience with the people in your life
so they may come to know Him too.
Talking about it proves you believe in Him.

* * *

AS A CHRISTIAN BELIEVER,
REMEMBER TO DO THE FOLLOWING:
1. Read your Bible daily
2. Pray to the Lord daily
3. Find and attend a local Bible-believing church
that will give you guidance, strength, and fellowship.

Made in the USA
Columbia, SC
11 July 2024

38223593R00126